May God bless you.

She
Worshipped
Him

Olive

She Worshipped Him

OLIVE GARDINER

AMBASSADOR PRODUCTIONS LTD.
16 HILLVIEW AVENUE
BELFAST BT5 6JR

455 GREAT WESTERN ROAD
GLASGOW G12 8HH

Printed in Great Britain by Ambassador Productions Ltd.

Contents

Dedication

To Averil who was in at the beginning
To the YWCA choir members for all their prayers and encouragement.
To Kathleen, my long suffering, travelling companion.

She Worshipped Him

Matthew 15

She came and worshipped Him
In her great need.
It seemed that Christ refused
To hear her plead,
"O, Son of David, help,
My daughter's ill".
But He continued silent
To her still.
And yet she followed hard
After the Lord,
Crying her need, and waiting
On his word.

"Send her away", was the
Disciples cry.
"I'm sent to Israel",
Was Christ's reply.
But still she worshipped Him,
And still she prayed,
"Lord, help me, help me please",
He heard her say.
"I cannot take the bread
From Israel's child
And give it unto dogs",
The Lord replied.

With these stern words the Lord
Seemed to withdraw
From this poor Gentile soul
Whose need He saw.
But still she worshipped Him,
And still implored,
Undaunted by the answer
Of the Lord.
"You speak the truth to me,
But dogs can eat
The crumbs that fall around
Their master's feet".

This woman's living faith,
That Christ the Lord,
Would meet her daughter's need
Had its reward.
"Your faith is great, O woman,
As you will,

Your child is cured of all
That made her ill".
And so, she found, His word
Had healing power.
Her daughter was made whole
That very hour.

She worshipped Christ the Lord,
Made clear her need
Until He answered her,
Despite her creed.
And we can know His answer
To our need
When we, in humble faith,
Draw near and plead,
Our souls must follow hard
After our Lord,
And worship Him, the true
And Living Word.

Time Enough

II Corinth. 6:2

There was a dream told, many years ago,
The dreamer? But his name I do not know:
Of how he dreamed of Satan on his throne,
His evil spirits gathered, all unknown,
A-waiting his commands, set to obey
His wily words, his wicked, sinful ways,
When suddenly, he asked, midst evil mirth,
"Who will go forth to ruin souls on earth?"

One bright young devil answered first, "I will,
I'll tell them there's no God", his voice was shrill.
"That will not do", said Satan gloomily,
"Men know there is a God to face some day.
They may deny it now, stifle the thought,
But when in sickness or to death they're brought,
Then deep within their hearts they know there's One.
That story will not lead them unto ruin."

Again from Satan came that question, stark,
"Who will go forth to ruin souls on earth?"
"I will," a second evil one replied.
"I'll tell them God exists", he said with pride,
"But that they're much too bad to come to Him".
"No, that won't do; their evil deeds, their sin,
Drives them to God. They've only got to read
His Holy Word to know He'll meet their need".

8

Once more the dreamer heard the question ring
Throughout the courts of darkness, "Who will bring
Ruin to the souls of men on earth?"
There was a pause and then a third stood forth.
"What will you tell them?" Satan questioned him,
"What will you do to help to ruin them?"
"Oh, I'll encourage souls", his voice was slow,
"I'll tell them there's a God that they can know".

"How will that ruin them?" his master cried,
"I'll tell the truth", the wily one replied.
"I'll tell them God, in love, has given His Son
To die for them and that each soul may come
To Him Who offers him salvation from
His sin — that it is free to everyone,
It is the gift of God and not of works.
Oh, they will hear it all, I'll nothing shirk".

The evil spirit added fiendishly,
"I'll tell them that the Gospel's true", said he,
"But that there's time enough to come to God,
To-morrow they can think about His love".
A murmur of applause passed through the court,
The Prince of Darkness, pleased by this report
Sent forth his evil spirit and today
Thousands are listening — "time enough", he says.

Only a dream? This plot was planned in Hell.
"Wait till you're older, you are strong and well,
No need just yet to give your soul to Christ,
Enjoy the pleasures offered, taste of life,
'There's time enough'," is whispered in your ear
When you have heard the Gospel message clear.
'Too late', will be the sinner's awful cry.
Eternal life is offered now, today.

I read this story in a tract and thought it would make a very challenging poem.

The Water Pot

John 4:28

She was so tired of all her weary way.
Nothing had changed, day followed after day,
The same old journey out to Jacob's well
In the hot sun; she found it hard to tell
Which day it was, the heavy water pot
A burden never shared, no cosy talk
With friendly neighbours, always there alone,
Never a word or smile on her way home.

Then came the day she set off for the well,
Unhappy, tired, her life a living hell
Of loneliness, needing, she knew not what,
Her soul as empty as her water pot.
And there, at Jacob's well, she met the Christ
Who was the answer to her soul's great thirst.
She took the Living Water from the Lord,
Drank deeply from the cup He offered her.

This woman met the Christ at Jacob's well,
And her first action was to go and tell
Her neighbours what had happened to her soul,
How she had found new life, had been made whole,
And at the well she left her water pot,
The symbol of her earthly sinful lot.
Old things had passed away, fear, sin and shame,
She'd met the Christ, would never thirst again.

Our soul's great thirst cannot be satisfied
By the delights in which the world takes pride.
We keep on searching for the 'something more'
To fill the empty place in our heart's core.
The answer to our need is found in Christ
The Living Water, bringing us new life.
Oh leave your empty water pot of sin
And find your thirst is satisfied in Him.

My Father Cares

Psalm 139

The hedges were high on the narrow road
Which led from the village hall,
T'was a lovely walk on a summer day
To reach my family abode,
But on winter nights, without any light,
It seemed that danger lurked
Behind every hedge and every bush,
Setting hearts beating fast with fright.

Many a journey from hall to home
Was shadowed by many fears,
And although imagined, those fears in my mind
Made me fearful of travelling alone.
Then such peace and such joy would come to my heart
When I'd find, along the way,
That my father had come to meet his child
And he'd hold my hand tight in the dark.

Many long years have passed and gone,
And with them my father too,
But I still remember the touch of his hand
When I was afraid and alone.
Now my Father in heaven watches my way
And when I'm afraid and alone,
He holds my hand and I hear Him say,
"Fear not, I am close, all the day."

'Tenderly He watches over you
Every step, every mile of the way,
As a mother watches o'er her baby
He'll be with you every hour of the day'.

This poem comes from my own experience in childhood. We lived in the country and many nights I was terrified, walking home from the 'Brownies'.

Poured Out

II Samuel 23:15

"Oh for a drink, a drink out of the well
Of clear, cool water there, at Bethlehem.
My strength is nearly gone, my thirst is great,
Oh for the water there, at Bethlehem's gate".

David, the king, was shut up in a cave
With many of his men, loyal and brave.
The town of Bethlehem was occupied
By Philistines, when David, worn and tired,
Uttered a cry of longing and of need,
And three strong men performed their worthy deed.

There, in the dead of night, midst all their foes
King David's loyal men crept on their toes,
And from the well at Bethlehem's guarded gate
They risked their lives to bring the king a drink.
His wish was their command and so they strove
To serve the master whom they greatly loved.

When David found out what his men had done,
The dangers they had faced to serve their king,
He poured the water out unto the Lord
And cried to Him in these heart rending words,
"Be it far from me, oh my gracious God
To drink this water, for it is the blood
Of these my faithful men, loyal and true,
So here I pour it as my gift to You".

David, the king, poured out this precious gift,
This water gained at such a risk of life,
For he had learned, midst all his strife and sin
That God was his Redeemer and to Him
He owed his all; all his obedience,
All of his love and all of his allegiance.

Our mighty Lord broke through the enemy lines
As David's men broke through the Philistines,
And won for all, our access to the springs
Of Living Water — Christ our Saviour brings
Through Calvary, His answer to our thirst,
His poured-out Blood — Water of Life — for us.

Disfigured For You

Isaiah 52:14

They shall see my Servant beaten and bloodied, so disfigured one would scarcely know it was a person standing there.

The fire spread quickly through the silent house,
The crackling sound of burning wood aroused,
From her deep sleep, a woman, beautiful
In face and form, a mother, by fear stilled
As death and danger crept on tongues of flame,
Licking the doors, cracking the window panes.
And in her room, a yard across the hall
Her daughter slept, her only child, her all.

No thought of self entered the mother's mind
As, spurred by love, she groped about to find
The bedroom door; the scorching heat and smoke
Blinding her eyes, making her cough and choke.
She reached her daughter's room, her dear child's bed,
Lifted her up and through the flames she sped
Taking them both to safety, unaware
The fire had scarred her face beyond repair.

The years rolled on, her daughter grew to look
As lovely as her mother had in youth,
But now her scarred, disfigured hands and face
Contrasted sharply with the young girl's grace.
They were good friends but neither voiced her thoughts
Of that one day when mother love had bought
Her daughter beauty, love and life,
And counted not the cost or yet the price.

12

They sailed, one day, upon a pleasure trip.
Many young people gathered on the ship.
Laughter and fun filled all the sunny hours,
But soon, the wind grew chill, the sun sank lower;
Her daughter sat beside a strange young man
Absorbed in one another, holding hands,
Not noticing the ship had reached the pier,
Her mother shivering in the cool, sea air.

The poor, scarred woman walked towards the seat
Where the young couple dreamed in friendship sweet,
Intending, in her love, to place a wrap
Around her daughter's shoulders where she sat.
The boy looked up and saw her standing near,
And in a voice, not meant for her to hear,
Said to the girl, "That ugly woman there
With the disfigured face, do you know her?"

Her lovely daughter looked her in the eye,
"I don't know who she is", and walked away,
Leaving her mother there alone, eyes dry,
Too hurt to speak, too wounded sore to cry.
Love to the uttermost saved her from the flames,
But she denied that love, she was ashamed
Of all the ugliness, the beauty lost
To save her life but at such dreadful cost.

Another was disfigured, beaten, killed,
Upon a wooden cross on Calvary's hill.
But man, to his great shame, has turned his back,
Denied the Saviour's last, great selfless act.
Love to the uttermost saved her from flames,
On each of us — we read it in His word.
For He is able — He has borne the cost
To save all men unto the uttermost.

He is able also to save them to the uttermost that come unto God by Him, seeing he ever liveth to make intercession
for them.   Hebrews 7:25

The Lost Coin

Luke 15:8—10

Anna was poor, a widow, all alone,
Her life was hard, she hadn't any sons.
None to support her, none to bring her joy,
She spent her days in seeking to employ
Her talents, so that she might keep herself.
She carried water, gathered sticks, but wealth
Was never hers, one only thing she owned,
Her precious headband of ten silver coins.

Anna had brought the headband from her home,
Her father's marriage gift, ten silver coins,
Her dowry, gathered at great sacrifice
And loved by Anna, not for its great price,
But for the treasured memories in each coin,
Her father's love with which two hearts were joined.
She'd kept this precious gift through all these years,
Through all the joys, the sorrows and the tears.

One morning Anna lifted her headband
To wear it to a wedding, close at hand.
She placed it on her head, then counted fast,
One coin was missing, Anna was aghast,
Where had she lost it? What was she to do?
Her precious ornament! her panic grew,
She searched in cupboards, underneath the bed,
She swept the floor, "God help me, please", she prayed.

The light was waning, darkness soon came down,
Still Anna had not found her precious coin.
Her grief was very great, her tears flowed fast,
She lit her only candle and it cast
Its feeble light into the gloom around,
And then she saw it, shining on the ground,
Caught in a crevice almost at her feet.
Her precious coin was found, her band complete.

A thankful Anna hurried to the feast
Her worries gone, she joined the wedding guests.
"Rejoice with me, rejoice with me", she cried
And showed her lovely ornament with pride.
"I thought my precious headband was quite spoiled.
I lost one of my treasured coins and toiled
All day to find where it had gone.
Rejoice with me, my friends, I found my coin".

Our Saviour came to seek and save the lost
By dying for us on a cruel cross.
For man has wandered far away from God
And all are lost, we read it in His word.
Our Father God's great love is shown to man,
The breadth and depth and length and height has spanned
In Christ, the gulf that's fixed by sin,
'Til man repents and finds new life in Him.

Likewise, I say unto you, there is joy in the presence of the angels of God over one sinner that repenteth.

The Hands of Jesus

St. Luke 24:40

"He's got the whole world in His hands", men often sing.
Those hands belong to Christ, the King of Kings.
Sharp nails were driven through them on a cross,
To hold Him while He suffered there for us.
God manifest in flesh, His human hands
Outstretched to every man in every land.
He has the whole world in His hands, 'tis true,
The King of Kings is holding on to you.

His hands were tiny hands when He was born
To Mary, on that cold December morn.
She must have kissed them as all mothers do,
Examined every fingernail and knew
Each crease and dimple of those baby hands,
As Christ the King lay, wrapped in swaddling bands.
The angels bid the shepherds go and see
Those hands which would be fastened to a tree.

His tiny hands grew strong until, at last,
A carpenter's fine tools within their grasp
He fashioned chairs and tables, mended ploughs,
Hewed timber into beauty, turning now
The hands which fashioned stars to toiling hands;
His workmanship makes perfect sinful man
That he might honour, glorify and praise
God's holy name, those toiling hands were raised.

The tender hands of Christ were often laid
In love upon the little children's heads.
And those who came for healing to Him found
Completeness in His touch and many, bound
By sin, received forgiveness and new life
And freedom from the hands of Jesus Christ.
Those tender hands have still their ancient power
To heal, forgive and keep us hour by hour.

The hands of Christ our Lord are cleansing hands,
Saving and cleansing us from sin's demands.
With those pure hands He laid aside His robe
And washed the dusty feet of those who would,
In a few hours, deny their Friend and Lord
And run away, by fear turned into cowards,
And leave Him there alone on Calvary,
Those cleansing hands nailed to that cruel tree.

The praying hands of Christ plead at God's throne
For all who call upon His precious name.
Those wounded hands, which bled for you and me,
While He hung there in dreadful agony,
Are raised in intercession for all men,
That they may all be one who come to Him.
And in those hands is deepest certainty,
A providence divine and majesty.

The hands of Christ our Saviour are secure,
For He has promised and His word is sure,
That those who love Him have eternal life,
Shall never perish in this world of strife.
And He has promised no one ever can
Snatch us out of His own pierced hands.
So, held secure, we all one day shall stand
Before our God —
Who's got the whole world in His hands.

The idea for this poem came from Mrs. Cowman's book "Streams in the Desert Sampler". The book was given to Kathleen Lewis by Mollie Trimble, the conductor of the Y.W.C.A. choir. Kathleen felt that the message would make a good poem. I found this poem difficult to put together but the response to it has been very encouraging.

The Good Samaritan

Luke 10

Sarah lived all her life on Albert Street,
From a small child the neighbours that she'd meet
Were her dear friends, each ready with a hand
When needed, always having time to stand
And talk, about the weather, price of coal,
Of food, of who was sick and growing old.
All a familiar pattern but now, changed,
Neighbours had died or moved, now all was strange.

People, with coloured skins from foreign parts,
Moved into Albert Street, changing its heart,
Its sights, and sounds and smells, all of them new
Made Sarah insecure; this feeling grew
As, day by day, she left her home to walk
Along her street, but, unfamiliar talk,
Strange words, assailed her ears,
She felt afraid but could not voice her fears.

Her daughter lived a long bus ride away
And Sarah tried to visit her each day
To help take care of Mark, her dear grandson,
Her fears forgotten when she left her home.
Those foreigners, Asians from Pakistan,
With their queer ways she could not understand,
But every night she said 'good-bye' to Mark
And hurried home before it got too dark.

16

One day she was delayed and night had come
Before she got the bus to take her home.
The street seemed shadowed, many lights were out
As Sarah hurried on, hearing the shouts
Of laughter through closed doors, music and noise,
Which drowned the footsteps of two vicious boys
Who suddenly appeared out of the night.
"Give us your handbag, Missus, and keep quiet".

Poor Sarah could not quite believe her ears,
"Now, don't be daft", she said, amidst her tears
"Get yourselves home to bed and let me be".
But she was punched and pushed, she could not see,
Her bag was snatched and she fell to the ground,
"Help me", she cried but no one was around,
So there she lay, bleeding and bruised, clothes torn,
She could not move — all she could do was groan.

Sarah despaired of help coming her way,
She could not raise her head, could only pray,
"Lord Jesus, help me", then footsteps came near;
A man across the street paused, thought, 'that's queer'
But did not stop, Sarah was left alone,
Her mouth so sore all she could do was moan.
Two older women stopped, "Just look, she's drunk,
That shows you to what depth this street has sunk,"
And on they went without a second thought
For Sarah, lying there frightened, distraught.

But help was close at hand, a car drew up,
An anxious face bent over hers, "Tut, tut
Poor lady, you're in much much trouble",
Sarah could only stare and groan and gurgle.
It was the man next door from Pakistan
Who gently lifted her and helped her stand,
He put her in his car, wrapped in a rug,
And drove her to the nearest casualty ward.

Sarah was overwhelmed by all his care.
Next day a card arrived with lovely flowers,
'Best wishes, get well soon' the message said.
Sarah could not believe the words she read,
She thought of all the times she'd turned away
Without a word when he had said, 'good-day'.
She felt ashamed, this man from Pakistan
Had shown her love — a Good Samaritan.

This story of the Good Samaritan
Was told by Jesus when a bright young man
Asked Him, one day, "Who is my neighbour, Lord"?
Christ answered him in short and simple words,
"Go, do thou likewise". This command still rings
Down through the years; to all of us it brings
Its challenge in our selfish, busy lives.
Who is my neighbour? Go and do likewise.

The first commandment says that you shall love
With all your heart and soul the Lord your God,
And after that your neighbour as yourself.
But we love Him because He first loved us.
Christ gave His life upon that cruel cross
To save all men from sin and death and loss.
He calls us all to love and follow Him,
Then we can all be Good Samaritans.

I read the story, from which I wrote this poem, in Willowfield Parish Church magazine.

The Trial

I dreamed, one night, that in a court I stood
Before a judge, in wig and gown and hood,
The room was full of people come to stare,
Curious to know why I was standing there.
I looked around and thought that I could see
Familiar faces, all were watching me,
And then, the judge read out, from a long list
The charge, . . . You're not a follower of Christ.

There, in my dream, I heard the judge's words,
"You are accused of not following the Lord,
You in the dock there, what have you to say,
How do you plead, not guilty, yea or nay"?
I heard my trembling words, "Not guilty, sir",
And all around the court there was a stir.
"What proof have you to bring, what's your defence?
Now call your witnesses with evidence".

I looked into the faces crowding round
And then a neighbour's frowning face I found.
I called her to the box, "Now, tell the court",
She'll give them proof I follow Christ, I thought.
"It is commanded that you love", she said,
"Your neighbour as yourself — or so I've read,
This woman in the dock has passed by me
Without a word or smile — no Christian, she".

Again I looked around among the crowd.
A coloured child came forward, crying loud.
"I was an hungered but no bread you gave,
You watched me on T.V., thought you would save
A pound or two, to send to Africa,
To feed and clothe that little child you saw
Starving, in need, but you 'forgot' somehow,
'Suffer the children' has no meaning now".

I looked, in panic, at the staring crowd
And saw my family sitting with heads bowed,
And to the witness stand I called my son,
Certain he'd tell of the good things I'd done.
"But, Mum", he said, "you always talk of love,
But you are often cross, impatient words
Are on your tongue, you shout at us,
Your actions hurt, you're always in a fuss".

I stood there in that dock before that crowd,
I could not look at them, my head was bowed
In guilt and shame, not one of them could prove
I served the Lord — I did not show His love
To neighbours, family, others in their need.
'I' was important to myself, indeed
My outward actions showed no inward grace.
The judge pronounced — I had not proved my case.

I wakened from my dream, a sense of guilt
Stayed with me through the night, I felt
Confused, afraid, where was my precious Lord?
I rose up from my bed, I read His word,
And then I prayed, "I will confess to You
My God, my lack of love; make me anew
And mould me in Your image, let me be
So like my Lord that He'll be seen in me."

Who Killed The Duck?

On Tommy's birthday he received a lot
Of lovely presents, one, a catapult,
His father warned him, time and time again,
As he played with it all around the farm.
Tommy enjoyed himself and he became
Quite a good shot, when he took time to aim.

On Tommy's father's farm lived four prize ducks,
The winners of a dozen silver cups,
Dear to his father's heart were those fine birds
And Tommy often heard his warning words,
"Be careful of those ducks, don't do them harm",
As he viewed Tommy's present with alarm.

One sunny afternoon Tommy went out
To play around with his new catapult.
The four prize ducks were swimming in the pond,
Dipping for food, tails in the air, heads down.
Those tails were his undoing, he took aim,
But all went wrong with Tommy's little game.

One of the ducks had, just then, raised its head,
Tom's shot was good, one of the ducks was dead!
It's lifeless body floated on the pond,
One of those ducks of which his dad was fond!
What would he do, the duck must not be found?
He dug a hole and hid it in the ground.

Tom's father could not solve the mystery,
And Tom hoped it would soon be history.
Next morning he went whistling to the door,
His sister called him, "Tommy, wash that floor".
He looked amazed, "I'll not, that's your hard luck".
She smiled at him and said, "Who killed the duck?"

From then on poor Tom's life was one hard round.
He washed and scrubbed and polished to the sound
Of, "Tom, who killed the duck, who killed the duck"?
He could not stand it, he felt he was stuck
In a bad dream, weighed down by guilt
And all because he'd fired that catapult.

Tommy was losing sleep, what could he do?
His life was not worth living and he grew
More and more guilty as the days passed by.
He could not go on living such a lie.
Grabbing his catapult he went to seek
His dad, heart thumping, knocking knees, legs weak.

Tom's father listened as his son confessed
That he had killed the duck, tho' he had guessed
From Tommy's manner many days before
That he was guilty; Tommy's heart was sore,
But then his father took him in his arms,
"You are forgiven, my son, do no more harm".

Next morning Tommy whistled once again,
His sister made her threats but all in vain,
"Dad knows I killed the duck, I have confessed",
And off he ran, no longer fear oppressed.
He'd told his father, he was free from guilt,
He'd be more careful with his catapult.

This parable of Tom and of the duck
Teaches a lesson while amusing us.
For we, like Tom, have tried to hide our sin,
But we are bound with guilt, we can't begin
To be set free 'til we ask pardon from
Our Father God through Christ His Precious Son.

I heard this story in Lurgan Baptist Church. It was told by Bill Kennedy from Scotland.

Jairus' Daughter

Luke 8:41—54

Jairus' little girl, aged twelve, was dying,
The doctors could not tell him what was wrong,
They did not offer any hope of healing
For this young child who had been fit and strong.
Her mother would not leave her daughter's bedside,
The house was filled with sadness and despair
This lovely child was dear to all the family,
Their hearts were sick with hopelessness and fear.

Jairus was a leader in the temple,
Respected by the rulers and his friends.
But now, his heart was breaking with this sorrow,
Yet he believed God would some guidance send,
He'd prayed throughout the long night for an answer,
Then came a servant with most welcome news,
Jesus of Nazareth, teacher, prophet, healer,
Had crossed the lake with His small band of Jews.

Jairus had heard the rumours about Jesus
How He could heal the sick, the blind, the lame.
Many believed He was the promised Saviour
Jairus' faith reached out in the midst of pain.
Was Jesus Christ God's answer to their problem?
Would Jesus heal their precious little girl?
He'd go and ask Him, now, this very moment,
"Lord, come and heal our child, Lord, make her well".

Jairus pushed through the gathered crowds with Jesus,
Who suddenly stood still along the way.
"Someone has touched Me, someone seeking healing,
Some person in the crowd is healed to-day".
Poor Jairus, anxious to keep moving,
Joined the disciples as they looked around,
"Many have touched You Jesus, pressed against You",
A trembling woman knelt upon the ground.

21

The Saviour listened to the stammered story,
Twelve years of sickness, loneliness and pain.
"My daughter, go in peace, your faith has healed you",
Then Jairus heard his servant call his name.
"There is no point in troubling Jesus further,
Your little daughter is already dead".
The dreadful words were like a blow to Jairus,
But Jesus spoke, "Fear not, trust Me", He said.

With Peter, James and John they hurried onward,
Around the house people began to weep,
"Why all this wailing, why all this commotion?
The little maiden is not dead, she sleeps".
The crowd laughed scornfully at Jesus' statement,
But, asking them to leave He took her hand.
"Get up, my dear", He lovingly commanded.
The little girl jumped up and walked around.

Her parents, overjoyed and full of wonder,
At Jesus' word gave her some food to eat.
He asked them not to broadcast what had happened,
Then left that home where death had known defeat.
Jairus' faith was tested to the utmost,
That agonizing wait, his daughter's death.
But Jesus filled his soul with hope and comfort,
Victorious life and joy rewarded faith.

In Jesus Christ we have the only answer
To life and death, disease and pain and strife.
A woman's hand reached out and touched the Saviour,
His hands reached out and gave a child new life.
Those outstretched hands are marked with cruel nail prints,
They're reaching out to save us from our sin.
Stretch out your hand to Jesus Christ the Saviour,
He'll lift you up, you'll find new life in Him.

That Day

John 11

That day will live forever in my mind.
Each time I look at Lazarus I find
My memory paints again those scenes now past;
The days of dreadful suffering and at last
His death, while we, my sister and myself
Waited despairing, having sent for help,
Not understanding why our dearest Friend,
Our Lord, was silent; why He did not send
Some word of comfort to us in our grief,
Or come Himself, His presence our release
From all the pain and sorrow of our loss,
But then, we did not know about the cross.

The three of us had lived in Bethany
All of our lives, a happy family.
Our brother Lazarus was dear to us,
Filling our home with laughter, friends and fuss.
Mary enjoyed it all and joined the fun;
But I held back, I was the eldest one,
And, I confess, my patience, often strained
To breaking point was lost, then I'd complain,
But through it all our lives were lit by love
For one another and for God above.
We looked for the fulfilling of His word,
The promised Christ, in Whom our hopes were stored.

Jesus of Nazareth had become our Friend.
Lazarus had met Him first and then
Had brought Him to our home in Bethany,
Where Jesus found renewal in our midst
And many of His followers came to hear his word.
My sister Mary always called Him Lord,
She seemed to understand, much more than I,
That He was special, but I always tried
To make our home a quiet resting place
For Him, when Lazarus would come with haste
To tell us He was on His way again.
Such joy was ours, but later came the pain.

It happened suddenly, Lazarus fell ill.
We did not know how sick he was until
The doctor called us to his side,
The shock so great we both stood there and cried.
But then, we thought of Jesus, knew we could send
For Him and He would come and heal His friend,
But there was only silence and instead,
When Jesus came at last, Lazarus was dead,
Already in the tomb for four long days.
We went to meet the Lord along the way,
"If You had only come he'd be alive,
Why did You wait and let our brother die?"

Our Saviour's love reached to us in our grief.
"I am the resurrection and the life,
He that believes on Me shall never die,
Can you believe this, Martha?" and I cried,
"I do believe Thou art the Christ, the Son
Of God and what You ask, it will be done".
We went with Jesus then to Lazarus' tomb,
Where we could not control our tears and soon
The Lord·wept with us in our grief,
And all those standing round in unbelief
Listened and watched as unto God He prayed
And called our brother Lazarus from the grave.

23

That day our Lord changed sorrow into joy
For Mary and myself, death was destroyed.
We did not know another day would come
When Christ, Himself, would rise up from a tomb.
We had to stand and watch our Saviour die
Upon a cross, there on Mount Calvary.
But, as He raised our brother from the grave,
So God raised Jesus up to be our Head,
Our Resurrection, our Eternal Life,
Offered to all men in this world of strife.
His Spirit lives in us, He sets us free
To live our lives in Him victoriously.

Now Jesus loved Martha and her sister and Lazarus.

Were You There?

Many were there that day when Jesus died.
They stood and watched as He was crucified.
The Pharisees and priests, glad to be rid
Of this 'upstart', Whose every word and deed
Had challenged their position and their power.
This Jesus would be dead within the hour.
He'd claimed to be Messiah, King of the Jews,
Now they relaxed, His threat to them removed.

The soldiers sat around and watched Him there.
They gambled for His clothes but did not dare
Divide His robe; thus prophecy, Psalm twenty-two
Was now fulfilled; God's word came true
Through men, whom Jesus prayed God to forgive,
While He hung there and looked at them in love.
Those men, who'd nailed Him to that cruel tree
Christ Jesus died to save, on Calvary.

Peter stood at a distance from the cross,
Ashamed of his denial, at a loss
To understand, how he, who loved his Lord
So much, in the priest's hall denied that love
And turned away and left Him there alone.
He, who'd protested loyalty, had sworn
Never to leave Him, he had run away
And left his Lord to die on Calvary.

Mary, His mother, watched as her Son died,
Her heart so full of pain she could not hide
The tears and sobs which shook her feeble form.
Fond memories filled her mind; the day that He was born,
The visit to the temple in Jerusalem.
She'd watched Him grow from boy to man
And draw the crowds of needy to His side,
But now, her Son hung dying, crucified.

John stood with Mary as the Saviour died,
His arm around her shoulders as he tried
To bring some comfort to her in her pain.
He heard the loving words from his dear Friend,
"She is your mother, take her to your home".
And, to His mother, "John will be your son".
The love of Christ shone from that dreadful cross
As they consoled each other in their loss.

The Roman soldier had seen many die
That awful death there on Mount Calvary.
But none had died as this man here to-day.
"Father, forgive them", he had heard Him pray.
He'd heard His words of love to the dying thief,
He'd heard Him speak to His mother in her grief.
The soldier's heart was touched by the dying Lord,
"Truly", he said, "This is the Son of God".

Were you there when they crucified the Lord?
Did you stand there and listen to His words?
Did you hear His 'Father, forgive their sins'?
Did you join those who jeered and laughed at Him?
Did you look up and see His nail-pierced hands,
His wounded side, head crowned with those awful thorns?
Did you see the love which shone from those pain-filled eyes
And hear His 'It is finished', as He died?
His love poured out to save us all from sin,
Come to the cross, you'll find new life in Him.

Matthew

Matt. 9:9—13
Matt. 28:18—20.

"And lo I'm with you all the days", Christ said,
"Even unto the very end". He laid
His pen upon the page and closed his eyes.
How weary he was now, how very old.
The years had gone just as a tale that's told,
But joy and peace remained in Matthew's heart
As they had filled it from the very start,
The day the Lord had called him from his desk
And then gone home with Matthew as his Guest.

Memory took over them in Matthew's mind.
As tax-collector in Capernaum
He'd had few friends, was hated by the Jews
Because he worked for Rome, and many knew
He wasn't honest, took more than was due,
And lined his pockets, taking from the poor,
His only friends were sinners, like himself,
Collaborators, hated for their wealth,
And so, his life was lonely, lacking love —
Until the day he met the Son of God.

Matthew had heard the rumours of the Christ
Who'd roused such anger in the Jewish priests,
Performing miracles in Galilee;
The paralysed made whole, the blind made see,
The lame was made to walk, his sins forgiven,
And Matthew longed to meet this Friend of men
Who seemed to be the answer to his need —
His need to be set free from guilt and greed.
Surely this Man called Christ could make him whole,
Could take the darkness from his weary soul.

Then Jesus came one day and Matthew met
The Son of God, there, on Capernaum street.
"Come, follow me", the Saviour said to him,
And Matthew rose, left all, his job, his sin
And followed the Lord Jesus in the way.
He opened up his home that very day
And with the Saviour as his honoured Guest
He gave a feast that all might meet the Christ,
The publicans and sinners whom he knew,
He wanted them to have this new life too.

Matthew remembered clearly how the Jews,
The Pharisees and Scribes, received the news
That Jesus was a friend to men like him,
Would sit and eat a meal with publicans;
And Jesus' answer — that He came to call
The sinner, not the righteous, to be whole.
Matthew remembered all the Lord had said
And done, in those short years before He paid
The price for sin, by dying on the cross
To save all men from sin and death and loss.

Matthew leaned wearily against his chair,
Re-calling, once again, the real nightmare
Of the disciples when their Lord had gone,
And their great joy, when, in the early morn
The Lord appeared to them in Galilee,
And said, "All power is given unto Me,
Go ye and teach all nations, baptise them
In God the Father, Son, and Spirit's name,
And lo, I'm with you always, with all men,
I'll be with you", He said, "unto the end".

The Upper Room

Luke 22
John 13

I've often wondered why the Lord chose me.
I wasn't one of the close band, you see.
In fact, I'd only come to love Him late,
I'd heard Him teaching at the temple gate
One day, His words just seemed to be for me,
He offered me forgiveness, set me free
From all the sins that burdened my sore heart.
He changed my life, He gave me a new start.
And every day my love for Him has grown
And filled me with a joy 'till now unknown.

Jerusalem was my home all of my life,
I lived there with my children and my wife.
We were good Jews, we tried to keep the law,
Observed the holy days and always saw
That all of God's commandments were obeyed,
But when Christ Jesus spoke to me that day
I understood, at last, what God's love meant
And that this Man, called Jesus, had been sent
To bring to all, forgiveness for our sin,
When we repent and put our trust in Him.

Jerusalem was packed with pilgrim Jews.
The feast of Passover was nearly due
When Jesus came to visit in our home
And asked me to reserve our upper room
That He might keep the feast with His close friends
In private — no one was to know, for men,
Religious leaders, sought to have Him killed
Because He spoke of God, against their will,
As Father and Himself as God's own Son,
Messiah, promised from of old, the Holy One.

Jesus and I agreed a secret sign;
His friends would follow, at a certain time,
A man, whom they would follow in the street,
Carrying a water-pot and then, they'd greet
Me with the words, "Where is the guestchamber,
The Master says, that we may now prepare
The feast of Passover He wants to share
With His disciples"? — all was set with care,
But I was ill at ease, I felt afraid,
Something was wrong — Jesus would be betrayed.

Christ washed the feet of all His friends, that night,
He broke the bread that all might have a bite,
"My body broken for you all", He said,
And then, they shared the cup, "I am betrayed
By one who shares with us". All of them gasped,
"Who is it? Is it I?" were questions asked,
And Judas, looking guilty, left the room.
I saw it all and knew that, very soon,
My Friend would die — this Man who'd saved my soul,
Had set me free from sin and made me whole.

The Lord has chosen you, as He chose me,
He'll enter every life and set us free.
He asks for the guest chamber of our hearts
That He might share our lives in every part.
His body, broken for us all, He shares,
His blood poured out for all in love and care.
Give Him that upper room, that guestchamber,
Give Him the right He has to enter there,
He knocks and asks for entrance to our souls,
That He may sup with us and make us whole.

The Boat

Luke 19:10

It sat in the front window of the shop,
Graceful blue hull and pure white sails on top,
The loveliest boat that John had ever seen,
Carved out of wood, its lines were long and clean,
T'would sail upright and fast upon the lake;
So John determined, there and then, to take
His savings from his box to buy this boat,
Among his friends 'twould be the best afloat.

The little boy marched in and asked the cost
Of that fine boat, he came out looking lost.
His pocket money would not ever buy
The lovely boat, poor John tried not to cry.
He stared at it again, yes, he could make
A boat as fine to sail upon the lake.
He gathered wood and tools and drew his plans,
Anxious to hold his boat between his hands.

John cut and carved and polished, 'till at last
His boat took shape; white sails upon her mast,
Blue painted hull and red flag flying free.
He took her to the lake, so proud to see
How upright, fast and gracefully she skimmed
Over the water; soon his joy was dimmed,
His boat had sailed far, far beyond his reach
And she was lost upon some distant beach.

John's heart was broken when he lost his boat.
He wandered home, dragging his feet and coat
And all the week was spent mourning its loss,
Nothing could take its place for it had cost
So much in time and love for John to make,
No other boat could ever take its place,
And then, one day, he passed the village shop —
There was his boat with the red flag on top!

Into the shop John went with eyes alight,
"That boat is mine, please, can I have her back"?
But he was disappointed, he was told
He'd have to buy it, it was to be sold.
John took on every job that he could find,
Ran errands, washed cars, did a paper round
Until, at last, he had the money saved
To buy the boat that he, himself had made.

John paid the price demanded for his boat,
He wrapped it carefully inside his coat
And hurried home, his face alight with joy,
"You're mine, you're doubly mine", he proudly said,
My own hands made you but you strayed,
I lost you for awhile but now, you're found,
I paid the price — to me you're doubly bound".

Creator God has made us for His own
To glorify His name we have been born,
But we have wandered far away from Him,
We're lost, astray, in this dark world of sin.
Our Saviour came to seek and save the lost,
He paid the price for us upon the cross,
We're doubly His — He made us, we were lost,
He bought us with His Blood, He paid the cost.

'For the Son of Man is come to seek and to save that which was lost.'

Abba, Father

Deut. 33:27

The sun shone warmly from a clear, blue sky,
The tall trees stood on tip-toe reaching high,
The hedgerows seemed alive with insect life.
And all around the fields of corn were ripe.
Along the road two figures came in sight,
A father and a child, flying a kite.

29

The kite rose up above the lofty trees,
Dipping and sailing on the gentle breeze,
The string was held with all the small girl's might,
The father's grasp upon his child was tight,
Laughter and fun filled all the summer air,
Father and child walked on without a care.

Then, o'er the sun, dark clouds began to form,
The wind made sweeping waves among the corn,
The tall trees seemed to sway in the rising breeze,
A rustling started high up in the leaves,
The girl held tightly to her father's hand,
As darkness seemed to creep across the land.

The dusty ground soon turned to muddy pools
As rain fell heavily, the air turned cool,
The road became a slide to little feet,
Her hands let go the kite and reached to seek
The safety of her father's caring arms,
Where she'd be sheltered, warm and safe from harm.

"Please, daddy," said the child, "please carry me,
The way is very slippery, you see".
The father scooped the child up in his arms,
"I've got you, darling, now you're safe from harm".
And on they hurried 'till they reached their home.
And found there shelter from the summer storm.

Our heavenly Father cares for every child
Of His, however rough the way, however wild
And He Who cares when e'en a sparrow falls,
Will stoop to help His children when they call.
His everlasting arms are underneath,
For Abba, Father cares, in life and death.

The eternal God is thy refuge and underneath are the everlasting arms.
My friend, Kathleen Lewis, told me the story of this poem.

A Little Child Shall Lead Them

Isaiah 38:17

A little girl, in Sunday school one day,
Had listened to her teacher, heard her say,
"When you confess and put your trust in Him
God will forgive His children all their sin.
And in His word we read this lovely fact,
God has cast all our sins behind His back".

30

The child's young heart was touched by what was said.
She knelt, that night, beside her bed and prayed,
"Lord, I am very small but I love You,
Please take my sins as You have promised to,
Put them behind Your back so I can see
There's nothing wrong between my Lord and me".

The little girl, excited, told her Mum
About the lovely thing that she had done.
"They're all behind God's back, it's in His word,
My sins are all forgiven by the Lord".
Rejoicing in the faith her child had found
She asked the question, "What if God turns round"?

The little one looked thoughtfully at her,
"I know that Jesus hears and answers prayer,
I know He loves me and forgives my sin
And God, my Father, looks at me through Him,
I've read it in His Word and it is true.
So, if God turns around, His back turns too".

Dr. John Girvan told this story to the children in Greenwell Street Presbyterian Church, Newtownards.

All Things New

Rev. 21:5

The garden was ablaze with tulips, crowds
Of lofty blooms of colour standing proud,
Flaunting their rainbow petals in the air,
Their loveliness revealing all the care
Lavished upon them by her mother's hands,
Among the many jobs which made demands
Upon her time — her little daughter's needs —
Refusing discipline for naughty deeds.

The sun filled garden beckoned to the child
Whose mood was angry, temper, short and wild,
Searching for something on which she could vent
The bottled feelings of her discontent.
She snatched some scissors from a kitchen drawer
And off she went; soon every tulip flower
Had lost its head; her temper cooled, she felt
Dismayed at what she'd done — consumed with guilt.

When mother found out what the child had done
Her hurt was hidden but her peace had gone.
Anxious to understand the reason why
Her child had acted so unworthily,
She took her little daughter on her knee,
"Why did you hurt the flowers and so hurt me?"
Her little girl put both arms round her neck,
"When daddy comes, he'll put their poor heads back".

So, sometime later, tulip heads appeared,
Much stronger than the ones that had been sheared.
Father had answered, lovingly, the plea
Presented by his sorry child and we
Who've sinned can turn to One, Whose love and care
Has blotted out our sins, made us His heirs
With His own Son, restored His beauty to
Our lives and, in His love, made all things new.

It was a great joy to meet while on holiday, Margaret Doe from Hornchurch, Essex, who gave the talk at the Sunday morning service in the hotel. In her sermon, Margaret used two illustrations which I have turned into poems — All Things New and G.P.C.

G. P. C.

A cotton-picker came to love the Lord,
Enthusiastic, keen to know His word,
To go to far flung foreign lands to preach,
To do some special task, perhaps to teach.
He stood among the cotton in the fields,
Eyes scanning feathery clouds which seemed to yield
A message to his eager mind and heart,
G.P.C. he read, then gave a start,
For in the sky the guidance that he wished
Was written clearly, Samuel, 'Go preach Christ'.

In his excitement, Samuel downed his tools
And ran to where an old man, keeping cool,
Sat in the shade of a banana tree.
"Look, look", he cried, "the letters G.P.C.,
'Go, preach Christ', the Lord has said to me".
The old man raised his head, 'till he could see
The cloudy letters, "G.P.C.", he read,
And looking into Samuel's face he said,
"I see the G.P.C. my dear, dear son,
To me it seems to say, 'Go pick cotton'.

Where are you placed? Where falls your daily lot?
In factory, office, school or kitchen fraught
With great dullness, day following dreary day
Where nothing changes, everything seems grey?
But we are told, in God's own precious word,
To do all heartily as to the Lord.
And God requires our faithful service where
His hand has placed us and we all must share
The gospel of the love of His dear Son,
He still says, 'Go preach Christ, Go pick cotton'.

How Can They Hear

How can they hear?
Their ears are deafened by their hungry cries.
Their bodies, swollen, grotesque, they try
To smile, while cameras click away
Showing their agony, a living hell of hunger,
Day by day, dying the slow death, bit by painful bit,
While we, the Western World, in luxury sit.
How can they hear?

How can they hear?
The Gospel of the love of Christ our Lord?
God's sacrifice on Calvary must be shared,
But how can people, young and old, whose ears
Are closed by suffering, hunger, fear,
Hear of His love unless they see it shown
By us, who claim allegiance to His throne?
How can they hear?

How can they hear?
In Ethiopia, Sudan, Peru,
Brazil, Bolivia, other lands too
People are starving, poverty prevails.
The answer to their need lies in ourselves,
The giving of our money, time and love,
Our prayers, as God has given us richly from above.
Then they will hear.

Count It All Joy

James 1:2a

How can I count it joy when every breath
Is choked off by the load of grief I bear?
How can I count it joy when tears stream down,
The house is still, weeping the only sound?
How can I count it joy when joy has fled
And darkness brings no sleep upon my bed?
How can I count it joy in all this pain?

But joy in Christ remains for God remains
Whatever be the circumstance or pain,
And He is still Redeemer and His touch
Of love redeems our grief, however much,
If we will pour it all — an offering —
Of love into His hands, then He will bring
His joy in pain, His joy in suffering.

These verses came to me from thoughts presented by Eugenia Price. They are dedicated to Pat Baines of Tilehurst, Reading. Pat, though recently widowed, is a good 'listener' and brought much joy and laughter to us during a holiday in Italy.

She Touched Him

Mark 5:25—34; Luke 8:43—48

Twelve long years she'd suffered
Loneliness and shame,
All her money gone now,
Nothing left but pain.
"Sorry I can't help you,"
Each doctor shook his head,
It seemed that life was finished
She must end her days in bed.

Many neighbours gathered round
When first she'd taken ill,
Cooking, cleaning,
Offers more than she could fill;
But the pain had changed her temper
And her tongue had grown sharp,
Disappointment made her bitter,
The future looked so dark.

Former friends 'forgot' to call now,
"Thankless task," she'd heard them say.
She'd forgotten God now
He just seemed so far away,
Too far distant to be caring
For a woman racked with pain,
Far too busy to be bothered,
He wouldn't even know her name.

So the days passed, all too slowly,
And twelve years had come and gone,
No hope left now, none to help her,
She was saddened and forlorn.
But help was round the corner,
It is true what people say,
That 'when you reach your tether's end
God meets you in the way'.

She heard the sound of knocking,
Was that someone at her door?
Painfully she struggled
From her pallet on the floor.
"Have you heard about this Jesus
The Man from Galilee?
He can heal all our diseases,
He can still a raging sea".

"Why don't you seek Him out now",
Said her neighbour at the door,
"He's coming through our village",
"But the crowd will throng Him sore,
How will I ever reach Him
How make Him hear my call?
If I can only touch Him,
It won't matter if I fall".

"Oh please, don't push so roughly,
Please, let me through the crowd,
I must get near the Master,
I've no strength to cry aloud,
One more step and I can reach Him
One more step — I see the hem
There, I've touched Him, oh, the freedom,
Oh, the freedom from the pain".

"Someone touched Me", said the Master,
"Someone has been healed today",
The disciples in amazement pointed
To the crowds along the way.
"Many, Lord, have touched You,
The people throng around".
But the Lord was softly speaking,
A woman kneeling on the ground.

"Go in peace, my daughter,
Your faith has made you whole".
She found healing for her body
And joy for her soul.
The future bright before her
She used her hours to tell
Of the day she touched the Master,
The day He made her well.

Many years have passed since Jesus
Healed this woman of her pain,
But the message through the ages
Hasn't changed, it's just the same.
You need healing, you need freedom,
You must forget your pride,
Just reach out and touch the Saviour,
Push your way right to His side.

Many women, over the years, must have wondered about this woman who touched the hem of Christ's garment
and what her life was like during those years of suffering. I tried to think myself into her situation as I wrote
these words. May all of you who read them find that her story is as relevant today as it was all those years ago.

Martha's Story

Luke 10:38—42

It was hot, that summer morning
In the town of Bethany,
When my brother came to tell me
That the Master had been sighted
Down the road, not far away.
"Martha, Martha", Lazareth called me,
"Do you hear me when I say
He'll be here in time for dinner,
He will eat with us today".

Yes, I heard him call that morning,
And I'm ashamed to say
That I didn't answer civilly
To his summons right away.
It was hot, you see, and Mary
She was out, I don't know where,
She was always helping others
It just seemed she didn't care
That the cooking and the cleaning
And the washing were all there
To be done, by good old Martha,
I was always there.

Well — on that eventful morning
I just had to start myself
To the cooking and the cleaning,
There'd be the twelve and then
The Master, Lazarus, Mary and myself.
What to give them, where to seat them?
Place clean towels on the shelf,
Leave fresh water by the doorway,
They'd be tired, they'd need to rest.
Where is Mary, is she coming?
Lazarus, call her, is she deaf?

Soon I heard the shouts of children,
They had heard the tramp of feet,
Is that kettle boiling, Mary
Have we prepared enough to eat?
But my sister too was running
With the children, there to greet
The disciples and the Master
As they turned into our street.

I confess it, I was angry
Why should I have to stay?
I was Martha, good old Martha,
Always there — I'd heard them say
"You can count on good old Martha
She'll feed them all today".

Through the window I could see them
Coming up the dusty road,
And my heart was sore within me
As I pondered on my load.
"The meal is nearly ready",
I could hear my brother say
As I placed the bread and fishes
On the plates upon the tray.

Where is Mary, can't she help now?
There she sits upon the floor
Listening to the Master's teaching,
I can hear them through the door.
"Master, I need help now,
Send my sister to my aid,
All sit down now round the table".
(One would think I was the maid.)

Then the Master turned towards me
As I frowned and fussed about,
And his voice came softly calling
Calming all my fears and doubts.
"Martha,. Martha, leave your dishes
Leave the pots upon the fire,
Join your sister, sit down here now
We will eat it by and by.
You have worked so hard, dear Martha
We will not forget your deeds,
But your sister Mary's wiser
She's aware of other needs,
You must feed the Spirit also
It takes time and prayer to know
All the good our God has given,
All the love he has to show."

Many joys and many sorrows
The Master shared with us.
Lazarus, our brother, died here
And the Master raised him up.
Well do I remember standing
By that grave upon the hill,
And the words He spoke in comfort
Are vivid to me still;

37

"I am the resurrection and the life",
He said that day.
And He proved it to me later
By His death on Calvary.

Many women, like myself, have been able to identify with Martha when they have found themselves in a similar situation in the kitchen, while someone else, who could be helping, seems to be sitting at ease. Our Lord showed Martha what her priorities should be. May this poem help readers to recognise the 'one thing needful' and to choose 'that good part which shall not be taken away'.

Naomi

Ruth 1 & 2:1—3

I have always thought that the story of Ruth and Naomi is the most beautiful love story in the Old Testament.
   And Ruth said, Intreat me not to leave thee, or to return from following after thee: for whither thou goest, I will go; and where thou lodgest, I will lodge: thy people shall be my people, and thy God my God:
   Where thou diest, will I die, and there will I be buried: the Lord do so to me, and more also, if ought but death part thee and me.

My daughter Ruth will wed Boaz tomorrow,
To me it seems to be a dream come true.
Tonight, my thoughts return to days of sorrow
And days of joy, although they've been so few.

We had to leave our home and go to Moab,
Elimelech, my husband and our sons;
My husband died, the boys wed Ruth and Orpah,
And then, they died, I thought my life was done.

Far down the years my thoughts take wing and wonder
At all God's love shown to the human race,
I thought my heart was almost torn asunder,
But God has shown me His amazing grace.

From Judah came the news — the famine's over,
Orpah and Ruth went with me on the road,
I loved them both, these girls who were my daughters,
I'd miss them when I left the land of Moab.

We kissed each other, eyes with tears o'erflowing,
Orpah returned to Moab, 'twas her home,
But Ruth clung close, with words so warm and loving
I'll keep them in my heart for years to come.

"Naomi, Mother, beg me not to leave you,
I can't go back and you go on alone,
I must go with you to the land of Judah,
Your people I will take to be my own".

"I'll live with you, Naomi, as your daughter,
And through the years your family I'll become,
I'll try to fill your loneliness with laughter,
Together we will make a happy home".

"The God you love I'll take to be my Saviour,
He's been your guide through all the passing years,
He'll keep us both in living, or in dying,
And each day we will prove His presence near".

Both old and young, we made our home together,
She gleaned the fields and ground the corn to flour.
I praise the God of Israel Who gave her
To be my daughter in my lonely hours.

He's led us gently through our years of trial,
God of the past, the present, the future too.
And now, my Ruth will wed Boaz tomorrow,
God's love is sure, His promised word is true.

The Three Trees

Tall and stately the three trees stood
Close together, deep in the wood.
Years it had taken to make them grow,
Sun and wind and rain and snow;
Now they were ready, these beautiful trees,
Dreaming together of what they would be.

"I know what I'll be", said the first tall tree,
"When the woodman uses his axe on me.
I'll be a cradle, carved and rare
To rock to sleep a baby fair,
A cradle fit for a royal house.
A beautiful cradle will be my choice."

"What will I be?" murmured the second tree,
"I love the winds that blow over the sea;
A graceful ship with tall white sails,
And a cargo of spices and silks in bales;
Facing the storms, sailing the seas,
A beautiful ship, that's what I'll be".

The third tree, tallest one of the three,
Looked over the forest to where he could see
Far in the distance, streets and roads,
People on foot, carts carrying loads;
"A signpost I'll be to point the way,
A beautiful signpost, for that I'll pray".

39

The woodman came and the three trees fell,
And what they became is the story I tell;
They had dreamed of their future, what they wanted to be,
A beautiful cradle, a graceful ship, a signpost clear for me to see.
They were cut, they were carved, they were hammered and nailed,
But what they became? Seemed their dreams had failed.

For the first tall tree was a manger stall
In a stable in Bethlehem town so small;
It was filled with straw for the cattle feed,
But once it fulfilled another's need,
And three wise men their gifts did bring
To the manger which cradled a baby King.

The second tree's future was spent on the sea,
As a strong fishing boat on Lake Galilee;
Owned by Peter and James and John
Who used it to fish in the early dawn.
And from it, a man called Jesus preached
To a crown of five thousand upon a beach.

The third tall tree was roughly hewn,
And dragged to a hill at Jerusalem
By a Man who was wearing a crown of thorns;
This was the purpose for which He was born.
And the tree was the cross, which pointed the way,
A signpost to all of Christ's victory.

Many young people dream of the future and of the form they would like it to take. These dreams do not often come true but, with the Lord as their guide, they may be sure that their future will be far more wonderful than any dream.

The Hungry Ones

Matt. 25:45

Did you see them that night, on News at Ten?
Caught by the camera in all their despair,
Babies and toddlers, old women, old men,
Framed on the screen, brought to us there
In our warm living rooms, as we sat at ease
Sipping our coffee, or drinking our tea.

Great eyes looking straight into our lives
From little skull heads, pot bellies, stick legs.
Hunger, starvation, before our eyes
In Karamoja, Uganda, they plead and they beg
"Give us something to eat before we all die.
Have mercy, send help", they mournfully cry.

Great black flies on a little child's face.
Three small boys pick dried meal off a bin.
The camera takes us from place to place
Showing more swollen black bellies, arms and legs thin
With hunger so raw we can't take it in.
One little fellow attempts a weak grin.

Did you see that programme on News at Ten?
What did you do, switch off, forget them?
Or did you miss a meal, count the cost and then
Send the money to feed even one of those kids
You saw starving and dying of hunger, in pain,
Or — did you do nothing, again?

This poem was written on Saturday, 7th June, 1980. On Friday evening, 6th June, 'News at Ten' showed a film
of the famine in Karamoja, Uganda.
I could not get the horrifying scenes of starving children out of my mind and felt compelled to write this poem.

The Feeding of the Crowd

John 6:1—14

My mother packed a lunch for me that day
I took my rod and tackle to the bay,
Five loaves and two small fishes in a cloth,
I was a hungry boy, I liked them both.
I climbed a hill and from it I could see
The clear blue waters of Lake Galilee.
The morning sun was warm, I cast my line,
It seemed to me that all the world was mine.
Upon the lake some vessels were afloat,
Among them was my Uncle Peter's boat,
And as I watched, he sailed it to the edge
Right underneath my seat upon a ledge.
And then around the hill there came a crowd
Of men and women, calling out aloud,
"There's Peter's boat drawn up upon the shore".
And as I watched, the crowd was swelled by more
Both young and old, sick, blind and lame
Streamed up the road, and up the hill they came,
All pointing to a figure on the beach
'Twas Jesus, they had come to hear Him preach.
All through the morning, afternoon, all day
These people listened, would not go away,
The sick were healed, the blind were made to see,
The lame man walked, the bound in mind set free.
The sun began to sink behind the hill,
Jesus looked tired and worn, but still
The people listened to His words.
"Lord, send them to the shops to buy some food,
They'll faint beside the way".

41

I heard my Uncles, James and Peter say.
But Jesus, in compassion, looked around,
"Bid all the people sit upon the ground
And you give them to eat", He said,
But Lord, we have no meat or bread".
I heard the Master's words from where I sat,
My lunch forgotten, lay beside my net,
I ran to Uncle Andrew and I said,
"Here are two fish and five small loaves of bread".
Then Jesus placed His hand upon my lunch
And lifting up His eyes to heaven He prayed,
"My Father, take this offering from this lad,
We thank You for this food, 'tis all he had,
Oh, magnify it, Father, by your power
That we may feed the crowd this very hour".
Then Peter, Andrew, James and all the rest
Took from the Lord the food that He had blessed,
And all the people seated on the ground
Received it from their hand and passed it round,
Five thousand people ate more than enough,
Twelve baskets, full of scraps, were gathered up.
The Master touched me gently on the head,
"You gave Me all you had, today", He said.
"If people everywhere, would give their all to Me
Their hearts and wills and lives, they'd see
My Father multiply the seed and pour His blessing
On a world in need".

I'm old now, many years have passed
But I have vivid memories that last
Of that one day, when, as a little boy
I met the Master and He filled my heart with joy.

Have you ever thought about that small boy who gave his lunch to Jesus? He must have been as hungry as any boy today who has spent a day by the sea but he gave all he had to the Saviour.
I pray that the boys and girls who read this poem will give their lives to the Lord.

The Dream

I went to church as usual that day,
I sang the hymns and also knelt to pray,
I listened to the reading from God's Word,
I heard it speak of Jesus Christ the Lord,
I saw the preacher climb the pulpit steps
The church was warm, I settled back and slept.

I stood inside a church in Nazareth,
I heard Him read the lesson from Easias,
I saw Him close the book and then sit down,
I watched the people sitting round Him frown,
I listened to their words when He had done,
They said, "We know this man, He's Jesus, Joseph's Son".

I sat among five thousand on a hill.
I shared the loaves and fishes, ate my fill,
I watched Him heal the sick and blind and lame,
I heard Him gently speak to all who came,
I asked of one who'd had his sight restored,
"Who is this Man?". The answer was, "The Lord".

I saw Him ride the colt from Bethany,
I walked beside the people there that day,
I helped to spread palm branches on the ground,
I heard hosannas ring from all around,
I asked, "Who is this Man whose praise you sing?"
They answered, "Jesus Christ our future King".

I found myself in dark Gethsemane,
I heard HIm pray in deepest agony,
I saw His blood drip on the ground as sweat,
I sat beside His followers as they slept,
He said, as Judas hailed Him with a kiss.
"Would you betray the Son of Man like this?"

I stood with Peter in the High Priest's hall,
I heard him say, "I don't know Him at all".
I winced as soldiers split His back with whips,
I watched as Pilate washed his hands of guilt,
I heard him ask his prisoner, "Who are you,
Are you as they accuse, King of the Jews?"

I saw Him drag the cross up Calvary,
I was among the crowd that thronged the way,
I heard their shouts and jeers as He fell down,
I saw the blood drip from His head thorn crowned,
I asked those standing near, "What has He done?"
The answer was, "He claimed to be God's Son".

I stood beside that cross on Calvary,
I watched the soldiers nail Him to the tree,
I heard him whisper, "Father, forgive their sin",
I saw the darkness fall and cover Him,
I woke and found myself there in my pew,
The preacher asking, "What is this Man to you"?

"What is this Man to you?" the preacher asked,
"Is He just Joseph's son from Nazareth?
Is He the One Who multiplied the bread
So that five thousand people were all fed?
Or is He Jesus, Saviour, King of Kings,
Whose death bought us forgiveness for our sins?"

She Loved Him

Luke 7:47

Simon had come to me, late the previous night,
With news of Jesus; He was coming back
To Bethany, our dearest Friend, our Lord,
Was coming back to us, He'd sent us word.
And so we planned a feast for all our guests,
Simon and Mary helped and Lazarus,
Whom Jesus raised from death to life again.
Jesus was coming here with all His friends.

We baked, set tables, worked all morning long
Preparing food; I did it with a song,
Because the Lord had taught me that my job,
Done cheerfully, brought glory to our God.
Mary, my dearest sister, did the flowers,
Patiently working through the hottest hours.
She'd turned quite pale when Simon spread the news
Of Jesus' visit to the waiting Jews.

Mary was sensitive towards the Lord,
She seemed to understand His every word.
Once I was angry when she spent her hours
Listening to Jesus; then, He showed His power
By raising brother Lazarus from the grave.
He wept with us; I saw His power to save.
"He that believes on Me shall never die",
He told me then; and so I love Him now.

Mary was quiet through the busy day.
She still looked pale, had nothing much to say.
The work all done, she slipped into her room,
I saw her lift her box of sweet perfume,
Her precious box, which gave her so much pleasure,
Her alabaster box, her dearest treasure.
Her tears fell fast, as over it she bent,
I moved away, not knowing what they meant.

Soon all was done, we hadn't long to wait.
The cheers, outside, told Christ was at the gate.
He entered Simon's house and took a seat,
Weary from walking in the noon-day heat.
We served the meal, and all enjoyed the feast,
I was too occupied to notice much
Of what was going on, or what was said,
Until a silence fell; I raised my head.

I saw my sister Mary just a pace
Behind the Lord, tears streaming down her face.
Between her hands her box of perfume sweet,
And, as I watched, she poured it o'er His feet.
I couldn't move, was rooted to my seat.
Mary undid her hair and wiped His feet.
Then Jesus spoke a quiet word to her
Before loud voices broke upon the air.

Judas Iscariot, not noted for his tact,
With angry words denounced the lovely act.
"This perfume, wasted here, should have been sold,
The money given to the poor and old".
Jesus looked hard at Judas, then He said,
"The poor you'll have with you when I am dead.
From this day, Mary's deed will be made known,
The world, much richer, by the love she's shown".

Mary poured out her all to Christ that day,
She showed her love in this, so special, way.
Her precious ointment, broken o'er His feet,
Filled the whole room and made her deed complete.
Have you poured out your all before the Lord,
Your precious treasures, all you are, in love
To Him, whose blood poured out on Calvary,
That we, to Him, a sweet perfume may be?

The story of Mary is told in each of the four gospels. Thomas a Kempis wrote-:
"Whatsoever is done of love, be it ever so little and contemptible in the sight of the world, becomes wholly fruitful. For God weighs more the love out of which a man works than the work which he does. He does much who loves much. He who has true and perfect love seeks himself in nothing, but only desires in all things the glory of God."

M. R. De Haan wrote:-
"Do you as a Christian attract others by your gracious words and deeds, and the sanctifying aroma of the indwelling Christ? The ointment Mary spent on her Saviour filled the whole house!"

Living Water

John 4:1—46

I had gone to the well, as I did every day
At noon all alone, 'twas the only way
To avoid the townswomen, their gossip and strife,
For the women of Sychar disapproved of my life;
They shunned any contact, I was left on my own,
So most of my time I spent in my home.

That day at the well I was happy to see
A stranger was there, He'd arrived before me.
He looked weary and tired when He asked for a drink,
And He was a Jew — well, it made me think:
It just wasn't done, Jews just didn't speak
To Samaritan women, and right there in the street!

He must have known, from the look on my face,
That I knew He belonged to the Jewish race.
But He spoke to me of God and His gift
Of 'living water', but His meaning I missed
For the well was deep, and He hadn't a rope,
Was He greater than Jacob, could He give me hope?

His words sounded strange as I listened to them,
He told me I'd never be thirsty again
If I drank of the 'water' He was offering me,
I'd be saved from my sin, I'd find I was free.
And then, He just seemed to look into my life
Said, I'd had five husbands, that I wasn't a wife.

Well, I thought He must be a prophet at least,
And I argued a bit about worship and such;
I spoke of Messiah, the One called Christ
Who was promised to make all truth plain unto us,
He turned to me gently and clear as could be
Said, "I who am speaking to you am He".

I set down my pitcher right there by the well
And ran through the town my story to tell,
"Come with me my friends, come with me and see
The Man called the Christ, Who knows all about me,
I have found 'Living Water', my life has been cleansed,
Come with me my friends, and see for yourselves."

The people of Sychar all flocked to the well
And proved there the truth of the story I tell,
They met the Messiah, believed on His name,
Their sins were forgiven, their whole lives were changed.
May you, who have heard my story retold,
Drink deep of the 'Water of Life', Christ the Lord.

This woman's story is familiar to us all. She must have been very lonely. F. B. Meyer writes of her, "One morning, when the land was carpeted with flowers of spring, a woman awoke in the little town of Sychar that lay in the lap of the twin mountains, Ebal and Gerizim. She little realised that that day would revolutionise, not her life only, but that of untold thousands. Throughout its happenings her story would be embalmed in the history of the race, and she would take the first step which, as tradition says, ended in martyrdom."
I hope that her story will 'live' for you in these words.

Bartimaeus

Mark 10:46—52

Day after day, he had sat there
In the dust of a Jericho street,
Blind eyes useless, but pleading,
Ears strained for the passing of feet.
Rags covered his poor filthy body,
Dirty arms reached upwards for alms,
"Please, help me", whined blind Bartimaeus,
But few coins dropped into his hands.

46

Year after wearisome year passed,
His pleadings were largely ignored,
People were used to his presence,
And he learned a lot from their words.
He heard of the deaths and the weddings,
Of whose daughter had married whose son,
He knew who was sick, or disabled,
But he sat there, blind and alone.

Then, one day, he picked up some gossip,
A tid-bit, beyond all belief,
For it had to do with Zacchaeus,
A publican, rich, but a thief.
Many a time he had passed him
On his way to the tax gatherer's seat,
But never a coin came from Zacchaeus,
Though he'd pleaded for something to eat.

Now, he heard that Zacchaeus was different,
Had changed, become a new man.
He'd returned, more than double the money
To people he'd cheated and harmed.
What had happened Zacchaeus?
A miracle must have been done.
Someone spoke of a man called Jesus,
He was there in Zacchaeus' home.

Who was this man they called Jesus?
The blind man sat in deep thought.
In some way He'd changed old Zacchaeus,
A miracle, yes, then He ought
To be able to help him, Bartimaeus,
Who was weary of life in the streets.
Who was this man they called Jesus,
Was it possible that they could meet?

Next morning he heard many voices,
Crowds shouting, feet running, much talk,
Again, of the Man they called Jesus.
It seemed, that today, He would walk
Right past poor, blind Bartimaeus,
Right past him, and out of his life.
This Jesus had changed old Zacchaeus,
He could surely give him back his sight.

The people were pushing and shoving,
How could he make his voice heard?
"Please, help me, Jesus" he shouted.
But the crowds only laughed at his words.
"Be quiet, blind man, you're a nuisance.
The Master has no time for you".
But he shouted the more, "Son of David,
Have mercy on me, please, do".

Amid all the noise Jesus heard him
The shrill voice calling His name.
And he sent for blind Bartimaeus,
Who arose, left his rags, and came
And knelt in the dust, there before Him,
His poor eyes, black as the night,
"What will I do for you, blind man?" asked Jesus.
"Lord, please, give me back my sight".

Jesus looked with compassion upon him,
This poor man, pleading but bold.
He spoke, in love, to him, gently,
"Bartimaeus, your faith makes you whole".
He lifted his eyes to the Saviour,
Darkness had fled, all was light.
And he followed the Man they call Jesus,
Who had given him back his sight.

Are you walking alone in the darkness?
Is each day a burden to you?
Cast your care on the Man they call Jesus,
He'll make your life over anew.
The Saviour will lighten your darkness,
He'll give you a vision that's clear.
The Light of the World has the answer.
Turn to Him now, He will hear.

The Cross Leads Home

Isaiah 63:9

Johnnie held tightly to his mother's hand,
Crowds thronged the busy streets, the shop was jammed
With jostling people, adults towered above him,
Pushed against him; he was sore in every limb.
"Wish mother would go home", poor Johnnie thought,
"Then I could play with that toy car she bought".

Johnnie looked up, and then he looked around.
Where was his mum? She wasn't to be found;
What would he do? She might be at the door;
Johnnie searched every counter, every floor
With no success, his mum had disappeared
And he was lost and feeling very scared.

The street was noisy, buses everywhere,
But he was lost and no none seemed to care.
He did not know which bus would take him home.
Johnnie was frightened, very much alone.
He sat down on the kerb to rest his feet,
Along came a policeman on his beat.

48

Johnnie gazed up into his gentle eyes.
He seemed so kind that he began to cry,
"Oh sir, I'm lost and no one seems to know
Where my dear mummy is and I've searched high and low.
I just can't find her. I let go her hand.
I looked all through the shop, then went to stand
Beside the door; it was no use,
I think she must have gone home to our house".

The big policeman took him in his arms,
Glad that he hadn't come to any harm.
"Do you know where you live? I'll take you home,
You'll soon be safely back there with your mum".
"Oh sir, my mother said if I was lost
That I'd get home by starting at The Cross".

Have you, like Johnnie, lost your way today?
Have you let go Christ's hand and gone astray?
You're wandering in confusion, darkness, sin,
The path back home is known only to Him.
In gentle tones He says, "My lost child, come,
Start at the cross and it will lead you home".

In all their affliction He was afflicted, and the angel of His presence saved them: in His love and in His pity
He redeemed them; and He bare them, and carried them all the days of old.

No Miracles

John 10:41

"The age of miracles is past", men say,
"The world does not believe such things today.
They may have happened once, not any more,
Men have outgrown these stories, this folklore.
Mankind is now mature and childish things
Are put away — no miracles today".

But — last Spring, from bulbs which looked quite dead,
Came snowdrops, white, with dancing heads,
And daffodils and crocus flowers
Of every hue, which show His power
To make anew from tiny seeds
Such wond'rous beauty — no miracles today!

But — last Autumn, farmers gathered grain
To feed the world, the sun and rain
Were sent by God to make it grow.
The farmer reaped it, row by row.
God can turn water into wine
And change the sky from blue to grey — no miracles today?

What do you say? Do you see miracles today?
A word from you, when used by God,
Can change a life, one only word
Or one deed done, can lead a soul to God's own Son.
Allow the Lord your life to fill
And men will see a miracle.

The idea for this poem came from F. B. Meyer's "Our Daily Walk". Reading for September 27th.

Footprints

Isaiah 46:4

His dream was vivid, every scene quite clear:
The Lord walked close beside him, very dear.
Before them stretched the beach of golden sand
Empty and silent, bordered by the land.
Across the sky flashed pictures from his life,
Many were peaceful, many filled with strife.
And, as they walked, he saw that there appeared
Two sets of footprints, his and his dear Lords.

They moved together down the stretch of beach.
The scenes still flashed before his eyes and each
Brought with it memories, sad or sweet.
And then, he saw that only one set of feet
Showed on the sand, the pathway of his life,
Just at those times when he had gone through strife,
When he was at his lowest and most sad.
And so he turned and questioned his dear Lord.

"Dear Lord, you promised me that you would stay
Right there beside me as I walked each day
Trusting in you and in your Presence dear.
And now, as I stand still and look back here,
I see, that at the times I suffered most,
The times when I was wandering and lost,
Only one set of footprints there are shown.
Why, at those times, did you leave me alone?"

The Saviour turned and looked at him in love.
Tender compassion showed in every move.
"My precious child, don't you know I love you,
That I am always close through joy and woe?
During those times you suffered trial and pain,
Those times when all seemed wrong and life seemed vain,
Those times when only one set of prints appeared,
Those were the times I carried you, my dear".

We are all faced with suffering in this life.
This land of ours is torn with sin and strife.
But those who love the Lord know that He cares;
His word says, He has made and He will bear,
That He will carry and deliver us
As, day by day, we walk in faith and trust
Close to our precious Lord we'll know no harm
For underneath us are His loving arms.

Broken Pieces

John 6:12

What are your thoughts, when you lie down to sleep,
At the end of a busy day?
How do you feel when you think of the things
You wish you'd not done and not said?
You started the day with a prayer on your lips
And committed each moment to Him,
But now, looking back, you have nothing to bring,
Only failure and sadness and sin.

"Oh Lord, I have failed You, again and again,
I started the day with such joy,
But somehow, somewhere in the rush and the work
I found only things to annoy.
I forgot about love when I spoke that harsh word,
I forgot to be gentle and kind,
I forgot to be patient with people in need,
Did not offer a helping hand."

"O Lord, I have failed to reflect You today,
To mirror Your beauty and love,
No one saw You in me as I passed on my way
Too busy to bring them Your word.
So now, at the end of the day, I'm cast down,
For I've no worthwhile offering to bring,
But I ask Your forgiveness, in His precious name,
As I offer, just these broken things."

Don't be discouraged, my friend, as you look
At the failures and sins of the day.
Lift your eyes to the Saviour, Who died on the cross
And has risen to show us His way.
He gathered the pieces of broken bread
He had blest that day by the sea.
Nothing is wasted, when offered to Him,
Broken pieces though they may be.

This poem was jotted down on the back of an envelope one evening in February 1982. It came straight from the Lord at a time when many problems were piling up.
   The idea of the 'broken pieces' was in my mind from the reading for January 25th, in Amy Carmichael's 'Edges of His Ways'.

So Are Ye In My Hand

Jeremiah 18:1—6

The people crowded round the potter's wheel
As he created there, with grace and skill
A vessel, beautiful in shape and form,
Before their eyes; a lovely vase was born
Between the potter's hands. His touch was sure,
Making from clay a vessel to endure.

The vase took shape as o'er the wheel he bent,
Steadily moulding, shaping, eyes intent
Upon his work; but then I heard a gasp
Come from the crowd and, looking past
Them, saw the new formed vase was marred
There in the potter's hand; we stood and stared.

What would he do? The perfect shape was spoiled.
The potter's perfect plan for it was foiled.
The vase, broken in many pieces, lay
Between his hands, just useless clay.
We waited, sure he'd cast it all aside
And start with new, that clay had failed when tried.

We watched; again the potter took the clay
Firmly into his hands and laid
It, gently, on the wheel, before our eyes.
Accompanied then by our admiring cries
That poor, marred clay was formed, by his sure hand,
Into a vessel, beautiful and grand.

The prophet Jeremiah, took a walk,
He tells us, down to the potter's shop
And there, the Lord showed him what we had seen;
A vessel, made of clay, which too had been
Marred in the potter's hand and made again.
"So are ye in My hand", the Lord told him.

"So are ye in My hand", said God the Lord.
But we, the clay, may thwart His precious word.
The hands which mould us bear the marks of nails,
And He will hold us, He will never fail.
He seeks to perfect us by His great love
Which worketh our salvation from above.

I find this passage very comforting. When we fail it is good to know that our Lord does not cast us aside as useless. He will perfect that which concerneth us. (Psalm 138:8.)

The Rainbow and The Cross

Genesis 8:9

That Sabbath morn was cool and dry and calm.
I went to church and prayed and sang the psalms.
The Pastor read from Genesis, God's word,
All about Noah's ark and of the flood.
He read verse one in chapter number eight,
'And God remembered Noah', was his text.
When Noah left the ark He thought of God.
We're told, he built an altar to the Lord.

Yes, Noah, after all the storm and flood
Remembered God as on dry land he stood.
He could have been so occupied with plans
Of what he'd do, without the help of man,
To build again a life on this fresh earth.
'Twould be a whole new life, a real new birth.
So much was to be done but Noah paused,
And offered a burnt offering unto God.

We're told that God was pleased with Noah's act.
It was, to Him, a fragrant sacrifice.
And there, God made a covenant with man,
That never, ever would a flood again
Destroy the earth; He made His promise so
That, in the clouds we'd see His lovely bow,
His token, set in colours in the sky.
His promise sure, He'll all our needs supply.

But, more than this God did for you and me.
He sent His only Son to Calvary,
His blood, the only sacrifice for sin
Can God accept when we return to Him.
The rainbow in the cloud, a promise sure
That seasons, day and night, will still endure
While earth remains; seedtime and harvest too;
God's word: each year we see it all anew.

William Wordsworth says in his poem, 'The Rainbow':

> My heart leaps up when I behold
> A rainbow in the sky.

W. H. Griffith Thomas wrote:

"While we do not always see a rainbow owing to the clouds hiding the sun, yet if we could get above the clouds we should see the rainbow on them. Thus, there is never rain without a rainbow being visible, if we could only get to the right spot to see it. But God always sees it."

Genesis 9:13, "I do set my bow in the cloud".

He Meets Our Need

Matthew 12:1—13

The synagogue was filled, right to the door,
With Pharisees and priests, with rich and poor,
All waiting in expectancy to see
Jesus of Nazareth: rumour said that He
Was coming to the service there that day
And that He'd passed through corn fields on the way.
The Pharisees were angry, said that He'd
Allowed His followers to gather seed
And eat it, breaking thus the Sabbath law.
So now, they watched Him, critical of all they saw.

There, seated in the midst, was a poor man
Who, all his life, had had a withered hand.
He could not move it, lacking any power
To lift it, he had suffered greatly, more
From taunts and jeers than any inconvenience.
He'd heard how Jesus healed the blind and lame, hence
His presence in the synagogue to see
If Christ would notice him and maybe He
Would heal him, though it was the Sabbath day.
Now rumour said that He was on His way.

He came into the church and there sat down,
Aware of all the Pharisees around
Waiting to see what He would say or do,
Trying to catch Him out on points of law.
But Jesus saw the man in all his need,
His lack of power, his weakness, and no creed
Or law could keep the Christ from making whole
A lifeless hand; He called this needy soul,
And stood him in the midst of all those men,
And, with a word, He healed him there and then.

Our Lord can see our need, yes, yours and mine,
It matters not the month, or day, or time,
Or man's objections on a point of creed.
He waits for us to recognise our need,
Our helplessness, our weakness and our sin
Which is forgiven when we turn to Him,
Who, by His death on Calvary's cruel tree,
Purchased our pardon, made us whole and free.
He meets our every need, He is our Lord,
Lord of our heart, Lord of our thoughts, and Lord of every word.

54

The Storm

Mark 4:35—41

Lake Galilee lay calm in evening light.
The last sunrays made paths, shining and bright
To where, with busy hands, the old men sat
Mending their nets, tongues occupied with chat.
Only the seabirds' cries broke the deep peace,
And gentle waves lapping the sandy beach.

Farther along the shore a group of men
Stood round their boats, they numbered nine or ten.
All afternoon they'd been besieged by crowds
Seeking the Lord, Peter and Andrew proud
That He had used their boat from which to preach.
Now, weary and tired, they pushed off from the beach.

The boat put out from shore into the deep.
Jesus, tired out, lay down and fell asleep.
Peter and Andrew, seasoned fishermen,
Anxiously scanned the sky for weather signs.
Strong winds began to blow, the sea to rise,
The sky grew dark, the waves increased in size.

Peter had never seen a storm so wild
Upon the lake he'd known well from a child.
Thunder began to crack and lightning flashed,
The boat shipped water, its useless rudder crashed.
There, in the stern, the Lord slept, on and on
The storm raged, the mast went overboard, the sails had gone.

Upon the mountainous waves the boat was tossed.
The brothers clung in fear, sure all was lost.
Then Peter found his voice and yelled his fear,
"The storm is raging, Master, do you hear?
Jesus, wake up and save us or we'll drown,
Oh, save us Lord, the ship is going down".

Jesus stood up and slowly looked around.
His eyes took in the sight, His ears the sound
Of raging waves, of roaring, mighty wind,
Of His disciples fear; His look was kind,
His voice was gentle; "Quiet waves, be still."
The storm died down, obedient to His will.

Peter and Andrew, their faces, pale with fear,
Stared at the Lord as, calmly, He stood there.
"Where is your faith, my friends and why this fear?"
The Master asked, "Why fear when I am near?"
"Who is this Man?" Peter was heard to say,
"Who is this Man the elements obey?"

Are you afraid when storms begin to blow?
Does your faith fail and drag your spirits low?
Do you forget that Jesus said, He cares?
He's in life's boat with you and waits to share
Your roughest voyage. He's there through good and ill.
In gentle tones He's saying, "Peace, be still".

The Saviour and The Judge

Romans 14:10

Traffic was lighter than usual
Down the length of the motorway
As the judge drove quickly homeward
After a busy day.
His thoughts were still in the courtroom,
Faces still crowding his mind,
When a car shot quickly past him,
"Young fool, he ought to be fined".

Farther ahead, on the highway,
He saw the same car again,
Swerving and skidding quite badly
And weaving from lane to lane.
"What on earth does he think he's doing?
He's driving like someone insane".
Then, the judge saw the car overturning
And suddenly burst into flames.

He stopped his own car quickly
And ran to the young man's aid,
He managed to pull the door open
Expecting to find him dead.
The man was alive and conscious,
The judge pulled him out of the car,
The young man was very grateful,
"You saved my life, thank you, sir".

Many years passed in the courthouse,
Then, one day, a prisoner appeared
Charged with the crime of murder,
The judge was one to be feared.
The evidence proved the man guilty,
The judge placed the black cap on his head.
The sentence pronounced was final,
"You'll be hanged, by the neck, 'till you're dead".

The prisoner spoke in a whisper,
"Do you not remember", he said,
"How you saved me from death on the highway
One day, when my car was in flames.
How can you pronounce the death sentence
On one whose life you once saved?
Have mercy on me", begged the prisoner.
The judge answered with words that were grave.

"That day, on the highway, I saved you
And gave you your life again,
But it seems that you didn't use it,
You've brought much sorrow and pain".
The prisoner pleaded for mercy
But the magistrate did not budge.
He said, "On that day I was your saviour,
Today I am your judge".

The moments are passing swiftly
And the Saviour is waiting still
For sinners to find forgiveness
At the cross on Calvary's hill.
But soon, this life will be ended,
Our Lord will be coming again,
If today He is not your Saviour,
He'll be sitting as your Judge then.

My Cross

John 19:17

"Take up thy cross and follow me", Christ said.
I sought, each day, to follow where He led.
The years flew past and with their ebb and flow
My spirit dragged, my burdens seemed to grow
Daily more heavy, there was none to care.
"Oh Lord", I cried, "this cross I cannot bear.
Why should I have to work so very hard
While others, rich already, reap rewards,
And spend their lives in happy, carefree ways?
No heavy crosses burden them each day".

Tired out, one night, I went to bed and slept,
My mind exhausted with the tears I'd wept.
My sleep was broken, 'till at last it seemed,
A vision formed before me in a dream.
I found myself where many crosses lay,
Some large, some small; I saw that each one varied
From its neighbour; some with lovely flowers, I prayed,
"Lord, let me choose my cross from one of these".
He answered, "Choose, my child, take any one you please".

I looked at all those crosses lying there,
And then, I saw one, beautiful and fair,
Studded with diamonds, rubies, set in gold.
"This I can wear in comfort, I can mould
It to my needs", I pondered in my dream.
I stooped to lift that cross, but then, it seemed,
My body bent beneath its heavy load,
I couldn't take one step upon the road.
"Oh Lord", I cried, "It's much too hard to bear,
This jewelled cross will weigh me down, I fear".

I looked around again and then I saw
Another, lighter cross, without a flaw.
Rich carvings cut it deep and flowers entwined
About its slender form; I could not find
One fault with it. And then, I lifted it.
That flowery cross, so lovely to the eye,
When taken up, drew from me a loud cry
The flowers entwined around it hid sharp thorns,
My poor hands grasping it were scratched and torn.
"Oh Lord", I cried, "this cross can not be borne".

Then, in my dream, I saw one, plain and grey,
Lying alone upon the dusty way.
No jewels shone from it, no flowers entwined.
Only some words were written there in lines.
I stooped to read its message from above,
A message written there in words of love.
"Take up this cross, my child, for it is yours,
Though it looks dull and grey and very poor,
I know which cross is best for you to bear,
I fashioned it with loving thought and care.
I bore my cross for you to Calvary,
Take up your cross and bear it now, for me."

I took my cross again from His dear hand,
It still looked dull, not beautiful or grand.
But, as I lifted it, a radiance shone
Upon it from above, its pain had gone.
It fitted my weak form, God made it so,
And in His strength I now, rejoicing go.
We do not know what crosses others bear,
We envy them, their lives seem rich and fair.
But heavy crosses are by others borne,
If we could choose, we'd gladly choose our own.

I read the story, from which I got the idea for this poem, in Mrs. Cowman's Streams in the Desert!

58

CHRISTMAS
POEMS

The Little Star

"But — mine is such a little light
What use am I on a dark night?"
The tiny star sighed to the moon
"What can I do, so small am I
Amid the darkness of the sky?"

The moon smiled gently at the star,
"Our God has placed us where we are
To do His will in every way.
We all must try, we must obey
Our Father God Who made us light
That we would brightly shine at night."

The little star shone happily
Down through the years until, one day,
He realised that his small light
Had grown quite strong and in the night
It made a path as bright as day
Down to the earth, a shining way.

The God of Heaven came to him.
"My strong, bright star, your light must shine
To show the world my Son is born
In Bethlehem town; you will make known
To eastern kings the stable bare,
And Christ the King who's lying there".

Our God has placed us where He will,
In corner small or highest hill.
But we must always let our light
Shine brightly in the darkest night.
Our light is Christ, Who died to bring
Light, in the darkness of our sin.

Jesus bids us shine
With a clear, pure light.
Like a little candle
Burning in the night.
In this world of darkness
So we must shine,
You in your small corner
And I in mine.
                    Susan Warner

The Spaceman's Christmas

T'was Christmas when the spaceman came to earth,
The world was celebrating Jesus' birth.
He parked his spaceship right outside the town
And then set off across the snowy ground
Towards the busy shops, the lighted streets,
The pushing crowds, with sore and weary feet,
Searching for food, for presents, Christmas cards;
The spaceman stood bewildered, looking towards
A great, tall tree covered in fairy lights,
Balloons and shining tinsel, making bright
The ground beneath, where stood a man in red
With long, white beard and cap upon his head.
He did not know what it was all about
And so he was determined to find out.

The littel spaceman stopped a passing man,
Arms filled with bundles, "Tell me, if you can
What mean these lights, this hurry all around,
These crowds of people, hither and thither bound.
Why that great, shining tree with all the lights,
That man in red, what's going on to-night"?
The man was startled and he turned to leave,
"Where have you been"? he asked, "it's Christmas Eve".
The spaceman looked in wonder at the scene,
"Christmas", he echoed, "what does Christmas mean?
I've come from space, I do not understand,
Please explain Christmas to me if you can".
The stranger led the spaceman to a seat
From where they watched the people in the street,

"Well", said the man, "at Christmas time on earth
We celebrate the baby Jesus' birth.
He is God's Son, His name Emmanuel.
Born in a stable bare, in Bethlehem.
An angel host proclaimed that He was born,
And shepherds worshipped, in the early morn,
The Baby sent to save men from their sin,
And so, we celebrate and worship Him.
The little spaceman sat and looked around
At all the shops, the lighted tree, the town
So full of noisy people, pushing crowds,
Street vendors calling custom, voices loud.
He turned back to his guide and sadly asked,
"I wonder where Christ is in your Christmas"?

Never Over

"I'm glad that's over for another year."
This is a phrase we very often hear
When all the Christmas fun has been and gone,
The crackers have been pulled, the pudding's done,
The turkey bones are soup, we're tired of cake,
It's time to throw the holly out and take
The garlands down, the mistletoe is dead,
Christmas is finished, the sales begin instead.

Christmas is at an end. Can this be true?
We've spent our time and money on a few
Close friends, our families and ourselves.
Unwelcome gifts are pushed to the back of shelves.
We feel let down, depressed, a sense of loss.
Completely unexplained, takes hold of us.
Is this what Christmas time is all about,
This let down feeling, this unrest and doubt?

Is Christmas time an end or a beginning
For you, my friend? Is Jesus Christ your King?
Or are you glad the festive time is only
A once a year affair, and months and days
Will come and go before you think again
Of Christmas? but, peace and goodwill to men
Is not the end; it's never, ever over,
For unto us is born, this day, a Saviour.

Christmas is not the end but the beginning.
The birthday of our Lord, our heavenly King.
God manifest in flesh for our redemption.
Salvation comes to us through faith in Him.
Down to a manger bed He came from glory,
The Word made flesh; we know the Christmas story,
Our Lord became a babe in Bethlehem,
New hope, a new beginning for all men.

In 'Share My Pleasant Stones' by Eugenia Price, the reading for December 26 gave me the idea for this poem.
   She writes: "There is no reason at all why Christians should be 'let down' on the day after Christmas. If we are, it is because we have allowed the holy day to become merely a holiday. We have centered our attention around gifts and family and decor. It is no wonder we are 'let down!' . . . Men and women everywhere (even Christians) sigh and say they're glad it's all over for another year . . . But it isn't over . . . It's just beginning! . . . Christmas is forever and ever because He Himself is the end."

Mary

Luke 1:2

It's quiet here in Nazareth, tonight,
As I sit, dreaming, in the evening light.
I can recall those vivid scenes at will,
My home, Joseph, the angel Gabriel,
The kind innkeeper there in Bethlehem,
The shepherds' visit, and the strange wise men.

Joseph and I had been engaged a year.
Our wedding day was drawing very near.
I'd been quite busy, getting all prepared,
That day the angel Gabriel appeared.
At first, I did not know that it was he,
Could not believe his message was for me.

"Mary, fear not, you are God's chosen one,
You'll be the mother of His only Son,
Through Whom men will be saved from all their sin.
Jesus, will be His name and He'll be King."
My cousin too, he said would have a son,
And she was old — God's gracious will was done.

Gabriel's message from Almighty God
Had come to me, it left me overawed.
But, all my life, I'd felt God near to me,
And, though I could not see how this could be,
I answered Gabriel, "I serve the Lord,
Be it to me according to thy word."

Nothing was easy after that strange day.
Joseph and I were married straight away.
The angel had prepared him, in a trance.
The village people gossiped, looked askance.
But God's great plan took us away from them,
We found we'd have to go to Bethlehem.

The government required that men return
To their home town to sign the census form.
We'd have to hurry there and find a room
Where God's own Son, Messiah, could be born.
I could not walk that long and dusty way,
So Joseph bought a donkey, small and grey.

That little donkey plodded bravely on
From early morning 'till the day was gone.
We got to Bethlehem by evening light,
I knew the Saviour would be born that night.
We went from place to place in that small town,
In every inn the answer was, "No room."

I was so tired I couldn't lift my head.
I almost didn't hear when Joseph said,
"The owner of this inn has a dry stable
And you may lie down there, if you are able
To find some comfort on a bed of hay."
God's only Son, my babe, was born that day.

I laid the Christchild in the manger there,
He was so little, beautiful and fair.
Even the cattle seemed to stand in awe,
Outside the stable shone a great bright star.
The shepherd's came, His birth by angels told,
Wise men brought gifts, myrrh, frankincense and gold.

So many memories, pictures in my mind.
Our flight to Egypt, 'twas an anxious time.
My babe grew up, a young man, fine and tall,
Almighty God, our Father, planned it all.
His name, Emmanuel, God's Son from birth,
My babe, His Son, the Lord of heaven and earth.

So many memories, joys and sorrows too,
Came with those words, "The Lord has chosen you."
God has His plan, I was His instrument,
An ordinary girl, through whom He sent
His precious Son to save all men from sin.
My Saviour too, all glory be to Him.

I have often wondered how Mary felt when Gabriel appeared to her with God's wonderful message This poem
is the result of such 'wonderings'.

Joseph's Donkey

The little donkey stood there patiently
As Joseph brushed his coat so soft and grey.
The stable here in Bethlehem was bare,
Only the breath of cattle warmed the air.
Mary was resting on a bed of hay
And in the manger stall the baby lay.

The donkey thought of home, his stable there
In Nazareth, behind the open shop where
Joseph did his work as carpenter.
He'd heard him talk to Mary, heard them share
Their plans to go to Bethlehem to sign
The census, Joseph was of David's line.

Joseph had brushed and saddled him that morn,
Mary must ride, her babe would soon be born.
He'd trotted gently o'er the dusty road
Making the journey smoother for his load.
The town was crowded when they reached the gates,
The inns were full, the hour was very late.

The stable of the inn was rough and rude,
The donkey could see all from where he stood.
He heard the wise men call the babe a King,
He saw the shepherds kneel and worship Him.
Of course he'd known, right from the very first
That God had come to live with men on earth.

He knew that Mary's babe was God's own Son.
Because God loved the world He had been born,
And that one day upon a tree He'd die
For men and women, such as you and I,
And that Creator God had made all things
To worship Jesus Christ the Heavenly King.

So now they'd have to travel once again.
For God had warned dear Joseph in a dream
That Herod planned to try to kill this child,
This little baby, born so meek and mild.
He'd carry them to Egypt, they'd be safe,
And one day they'd go home to Nazareth.

We accept as 'gospel' the idea that Joseph and Mary travelled by donkey from Nazareth to Bethlehem, although
this is not stated in the New Testament. I hope you enjoy this poem written from the 'donkey's' point of view.

Candles at Christmas

What would Christmas be like without candles?
Have you ever considered the thought?
Are you young enough still to remember the thrill
You got as a child, when you caught your first sight
Of the lights on the tree and the windowsill?

What would we do without candles?
The shadowy glow of their light.
The reds and the blues, the greens and the white,
In clusters on tables they make quite a sight.
At Christmas we'd miss their soft light.

In the beginning, God made the light.
With care He divided the day from the night.
The sun and the moon, the stars in the sky,
All created in love for man to enjoy,
The light in the world, and the light in man's eye.

But man in his folly brought darkness to earth,
And sin in man's soul meant sorrow and death,
Then God showed His love in a baby's birth,
A star showed the way to the manger stall
Where the Light of the World was born for us all.

So this Christmas time when the candles glow,
Remember the lesson the candle light shows
In the carols we sing, and the joy we bestow,
We are lights in the world to show men the way
To the Light of the World born on Christmas Day.

When I think of candlelight at Christmas time I remember this story.
   During the 1914—18 war people, in America, who had had a son killed, put a candle in the window as a sign that they had given him for their country. A child, seeing the evening star alone in the sky, was heard to say that God must have given His Son to die for the world because His 'candle' was shining brightly above.

The Shepherd's Story

Luke 2:8—20

Today I saw the man called Jesus die.
I heard the angry crowd roar, "Crucify".
I saw His mother Mary stand and weep
Beneath the cross on Calvary's hill, so steep.
And memories, undimmed with passing years
Returned to me, and filled my heart with tears.

That night upon the hill was dark and cold.
The sheep were safely gathered in the fold.
My father and my brothers were asleep,
I was on watch, my turn to guard the sheep.
I huddled closer to the dying fire,
And then, my eye was caught by one bright star.

It hung there, low in the mid-night sky,
It seemed to beckon me, I wondered why,
And then I heard sweet singing far away,
I looked around, the night was bright as day.
I woke my family and we stared in fear
As angels voices rang out, strong and clear.

One heavenly being, brighter than all the rest,
Spoke to us gently, as in fear we pressed
Closely together on the stony hill.
"Fear not, you shepherds, joyful news I bring
To thrill the hearts of men, now, and in years to come.
Glad news, of One, a Baby, born to be King".

The angel told us of a Saviour's birth,
That God had come to live with men on earth,
That down in David's city was a stall
Cradling a baby, born to save us all.
The star would show us where the baby lay
In swaddling bands among the dusty hay.

A multitude of angels joined in songs
Of praise to God, and then departed.
All was still; we looked at one another.
Father said, "Let's go and see this baby
Born today, the shining star
Will guide us on our way".

We reached the stable, rough it was and bare.
I entered first, and saw His mother Mary,
Fair and lovely as she bent over the baby,
Joseph stood by, the scent of cattle
Mingled with the hay. We stood in awe,
And then we kneeled to pray.

So many years ago. I heard of Him,
And saw Him grow from youth to man and draw
The crowds of needy to His side.
Today I heard the crowds cry, "Crucify".
He was that baby of Whose birth the angels told
That night I kept my watch beside the fold.

Perhaps it is unusual to begin a Christmas poem with a 'picture' of the crucifixion, but, as Jesus was born to die on the cross, we cannot separate the two events.
  I think that Luke 2:8—16, in the words of the Authorised Version, is pure poetry.

*

Another way

Matthew 2:12

Watching the star, the Wisemen travelled on,
O'er rough and smooth, it led them, far from home.
Long months had passed since first they'd seen its light,
And learned the meaning, heralded by its sight.
A Prince was born, in lands far to the west,
Somewhere in Jewish country, was their guess.

Their journey took them over hill and vale,
Through deserts, sandstorms, pleasant winds and gales.
A baby Prince was born in Israel,
Promised of old, His name, Emmanuel,
A holy child, Messiah come to earth
To save the world; the reason for His birth.

They thought He's be in royal splendour laid,
In silken robes, soft blankets for His bed.
But not in royal palace was He found
But in a simple home in Bethelehem town.
They brought their gifts and laid before Him there,
Perfume of frankincense and gold and myrrh.

The star had guided all along the way
To this small child, on this momentous day.
Their hearts were touched with love and joy anew,
Faith in the baby, Jesus the Saviour, grew.
Then, in a dream, they heard God's message say,
"Return now to your homes another way".

The Wisemen sought and found the Son of God,
The Saviour of the world, Jesus the Lord.
And they returned, rejoicing, day by day.
They took another road, another way.
Life changed for them that day in Bethlehem,
They found the Lord and knelt and worshipped Him.

When we find Christ, we take another road.
We follow His directions, trust His word.
Forgetting things behind, we reach ahead,
He is our star, we go where we are led.
His Presence going with us every day,
As we step out upon another way.

At the beginning of each year many people make New Year resolutions about changing their lives, taking a new way. Usually these self promises are forgotten very quickly.
Jesus said, "I am the way". John 14:6.

If Christ Had Not Come

The presents were wrapped, the stockings hung up,
The Christmas tree sparkling, the angel on top.
Garlands were hanging from ceiling and walls
With mistletoe, holly and silver balls.
The logs on the fire gave out glowing heat,
The scents from the kitchen spoke of good things to eat.
I leaned back in my chair and thought of the morn,
'Twould be Christmas day, when the Christchild was born.

I slept, and I dreamed I had awakened to see
That the room was all bare, there was no Christmas tree,
No presents, no stockings, the lights had all gone,
No knowledge of Jesus, He hadn't been born.
There wasn't a church outside in the street,
No loving fellowship, no friends to greet.
I went to my study and found, as I feared,
The books about Jesus had all disappeared.

A ring at the door, a small boy stood there
Sobbing and crying about his mother.
Would I come and visit? The woman was ill.
I opened my Bible, and sat very still,
For, the gospels were missing, I couldn't give her
A real word of comfort about a Saviour.
No promise of hope, no glory to share.
I sat by her bed, head bowed in despair.

Later that week, I stood by her grave
With no word to console, no word that could save,
No resurrection, no glorious heaven,
No joyous reunion, no blessing given.
I wept, in my dream, such hot, bitter tears,
As I realised then that He was not here.
Christ had not come, He hadn't been born.
There was no Christmas Eve and no Christmas morn.

I awoke with a start and a great flood of praise
Filled my whole being, for voices were raised
In glorious harmony, there, in my church,
In a beautiful carol I loved very much.
'O, come all ye faithful', the church bells rang out.
My heart lifted in joy, I gave a great shout,
"O, come and behold Him, for born is God's Son,
O, let us adore Him, Christ Jesus has come."

When looking for new ideas for Christmas poems I read the story, from which I wrote this poem, in 'Streams in the Desert' by Mrs. Cowman. I found the idea very thought provoking and the poem was very warmly received during the 1981 Christmas period.

'A few years ago a striking Christmas card was published, with this title, "If Christ had not come". It was founded upon our Saviour's words, "If I had not come". The card represented a clergyman falling into a short sleep in his study on Christmas morning and dreaming of a world into which Jesus had never come.'

The Star

Matt. 2:2

Darkness fell quickly o'er the land that night,
O'er rugged hills outlined in the evening light.
In Bethlehem the wind howled in the streets,
Crowds hurried home to warmth and food to eat,
All of them busy, none to lift an eye
To where a star shone in the evening sky.
Their doors were closed, no room, no bed to spare
For any stranger late, and none to care.

Way out along the road from Nazareth
A donkey plodded slowly in the dust,
Upon his back, weary and tired, there rode
A woman, and in front a tall man strode,
Leading the donkey gently on his way.
Would they arrive before the end of day?
There, in the sky, a star hung, shining, bright
Guiding the weary travellers by it's light.

Where would they rest that night, was Joseph's thought.
The crowds had left them far behind; he really ought
To have remembered Mary's plight,
But now they would arrive late in the night,
Where would he find a shelter for her need?
The shining star above them seemed to lead
Them, would it point the way to where God's Son,
The infant Saviour, Jesus, would be born?

Down in the shepherd's fields, the wind blew cold.
Huddled around the fire, men young and old
Wrapped in their heavy cloaks, guarding the sheep,
Sat in deep thought, while others lay asleep.
Saw the bright star as o'er the town it hung,
Heard the sweet song by choirs of angels sung,
Listened in awe to news of Jesus' birth,
A Saviour come to live with men on earth.

Far in the desert, kings on camels rode
Eyes following the star, as its light showed
Clear in the night the way the men should go.
A baby King was born, they did not know
That Herod's palace was not where He lay,
But in a stable nestled in the hay.
The holy Child, God's Son, was lowly born.
The star proclaimed His birth that early morn.

Mary and Joseph, the shepherds and the kings
All saw the star and heard it's message bring
Joy to the world, and love and peace on earth,
The wond'rous story of the Saviour's birth.
But as in Bethlehem, so we today
Selfishly busy, do not see the way
The shining star still leads at Christmas tide.
We shut our hearts to those who are outside,
The strangers, lonely, lost, for whom Christ died.

Although the star is only mentioned in St. Matthew's gospel in connection with the Wise Men, many others may
have seen it as well. May we all remember the message of 'The Star' when the excitement of Christmas has vanished.

The Innkeeper Remembers

I remember well, that evening,
We were busy as could be,
All our rooms were overflowing,
Bethlehem was full, you see,
For the Roman census taking,
When our servant said to me,
"There's a couple, with a donkey,
Asking for you urgently".

I remember how, that evening
When I saw them at the door,
When I had to tell them, "Sorry,
There's no room for any more",
That a great, bright star was shining,
And it seemed to hang right o'er
The rooftop of our stable.
And my heart was very sore.

I remember Joseph pleading,
Mary looking tired and worn.
The donkey standing patiently.
My heart was touched and torn
When Joseph whispered softly,
"Soon her baby will be born".
I just had to give them shelter
From the bitter cold and storm.

I remember, as I showed them
To the stable in the yard,
That bright star still stood over head
As if it was on guard;
The air was warm inside the stable,
The cattle safely in their shed.
Joseph pulled hay from the manger
And spread it out for Mary's bed.

I remember clearly also
When the Baby boy was born,
How some shepherds from the hillside
Knelt in worship in the dawn.
Told us of the angels' singing,
Of the message of His birth
Brought to simple men, glad tidings,
Joy to all and peace on earth.

I remember too, the evening
When some wise men from afar
Enquired about the Baby,
Said they'd followed a bright star.
I saw them kneel before Him,
And spread gifts before Him there,
Mary showed them to me later,
Gold and frankincense and myrrh.

I often think, as I remember
All that happened here that night,
That I could have missed the Saviour
If I'd kept the door shut tight.
So, may each of you remember,
As you celebrate His birth,
To open your heart's door to Jesus
That you may know His peace on earth.

Luke 2:7 reads, 'And she brought forth her firstborn son, and wrapped him in swaddling clothes, and laid him in a manger; because there was no room for them in the inn!

We think of the manger as belonging to the inn and so, for this poem, I thought of the innkeeper taking an interest in the couple, the Baby and the happenings of that night.

EASTER
POEMS

The Garden

There, in the morning light, the city lay
Golden and gleaming, in the hot sun's rays.
The streets, already packed with busy crowds,
Arabs and Jews, crying their wares aloud.
Gentiles from many lands on pilgrimage
To this, the Holy City, to this stage
On which, Jesus, God's only Son was slain,
Buried in Joseph's tomb, and rose again.

Jerusalem's dusty streets were filled with noise.
Veiled Arab women, heavy baskets poised
On covered heads, went on their way.
Beggars, with outstretched hands, day after day
Lining the filthy streets, and over all
The spicy smells of food on many stalls
Mixed with the fumes of petrol in the air
From cars and buses, racing here and there.

I left the noisy crowds, the busy street,
The beggars, sitting in the burning heat,
And through a door, set in a high stone wall,
Entered a quiet garden where trees, tall
And stately stood, their shadows on the ground
Making cool resting places all around.
A small bird sang, high on a branch, somewhere.
Perfume from many flowers, filled the warm air.

I took a seat under a shady tree.
I felt as if the silence spoke to me.
The air seemed holy, full of quiet peace.
It was as though the outside world had ceased
To be, and there I sat, in contemplation lost,
For this was Calvary's garden of the cross.
I could see Golgotha, that place of doom,
And there, beyond the trees, the empty tomb.

Wrapped in that beauty, pictures filled my mind.
I heard the soldier's laughter and the grind
Of that great stone they rolled before the door.
Joseph, who owned the garden, stood there too
Head bowed in sorrow; I could see a few
Veiled women, hear their sobs filling the air.
All seemed so real I felt that I was there.

The picture changed again; the mists of dawn
Were cleared away; 'twas early morn
When, through the trees, a weeping woman moved.
I saw her face, its ravaged features proved
Her tears were for the One within the grave.
Then, suddenly, they changed, she looked amazed,
Then puzzled; wonder and joy lit up her face,
Where that great stone had been was empty space.

Among the trees Another then appeared.
The woman turned about as if in fear,
But some familiar movement caught her eye,
She fell upon her knees, I heard her cry,
"Rabboni, Master, is it really You?"
"Mary", He said, and with those words I knew
That, in imagination, I had been
A silent witness to that sacred scene.

The silence in the garden kept me still
Sitting in contemplation there, until
It seemed to me, a touch, lighter than air,
More gentle than a breeze, brushed o'er my hair.
I heard my name whispered in loving tones,
"My child, I am alive, and you are not alone,
I rose, victorious, from that empty grave,
My blood was shed a sinful world to save."

I left that quiet place, that empty tomb,
I left the golden city, travelled home
To mundane tasks and ordinary ways.
But often, in the passing of the days,
I feel that touch again, hear that dear voice
Speaking my name, "My child, rejoice
In Me". Again He says, in loving tones,
"I've risen, I'm alive, you're not alone".

In August 1980 we spent two memorable weeks in Israel. The beauty of the garden at Gordon's Calvary, considered
by many Christians to be the true site of Christ's death, burial and resurrection, inspired this poem.

Mary's Thoughts on Good Friday

John 19:25—27

The room is dark and all is quiet now,
I am alone and lonely in my grief
So much has happened — if my thoughts allow
I'll tell you of my Son — words bring relief
And memories are dear.

What did I think as on that hill I stood
Amid the crowd who'd come to mock and taunt
My Son upon the cross? Their words were rude,
Their faces filled with hate — enough to daunt
The strongest of His friends — and we were weak.

This is my Son, I see Him hanging there,
Yet can't believe that all has come to pass.
The angel Gabriel said a son I'd bear,
Old Simeon said, "A sword shall pierce thy soul", alas
And now it's happened.

I gave Him birth in Bethlehem's stable cold,
The shepherds knelt, and wisemen from the east, in worship.
Then came an angel once again and told us
To flee with Him to Egypt.
Then we went home to Nazareth.

For thirty years I knew Him as my Son,
Yet not mine, He was the Son of God in human frame.
He helped dear Joseph 'till the work was done,
Then off He'd go to help the sick and lame,
His thoughts always of others.

We had a wedding once in Cana, Galilee,
He too was there, He loved to join the fun,
The wine ran short, the servants came to me,
I told my Son, He spoke, and it was done.
The wine poured out in love.

Three short years, He gave to all in need,
His twelve disciples followed in His way,
Love for the Father, love in word and deed,
"Forgive, forgive", was what He used to say,
And now they've silenced Him.

Today I stood and watched him crucified,
He thought of me and bade John take me home,
"Forgive them, God", He whispered, then He died,
And now I'm here — it's dark and I'm alone
Without my Son.

Have you ever taken the time to think of what our Lord's mother suffered when He was crucified? We know that she stood with the other women at the cross. May I take you, in imagination, into her home on the evening of the crucifixion?

Mary's Thoughts on Easter Sunday

John 20

Three days ago I sat alone and cried,
My Son was dead, the future looked so black,
His friends had scattered, each thought,
"He is dead, I must go back, back to the sea
From where He first called me".

Now all has changed, my heart is full of praise.
We took the spices, early in the morning
Down to the grave and there we stood, amazed.
The stone was rolled away, and in the dawning
An angel spoke to us these words of cheer,
"Fear not, you women, He you came to seek is gone,
He's risen, He's not here".

Yes, He had told us He would rise again,
I should have known they could not kill God's Son.
He showed Himself to us — He looked the same,
Yet not the same, the marks of what was done
Upon His hands and in His side,
He is alive, my Son, my King,
He is alive.

This poem follows the previous one as spring follows winter.
Between Good Friday and Easter Sunday the women and the disciples were in despair, but Jesus rose from the grave and brought hope, joy and life to them and to all who through the years, have trusted Him.
I hope this poem gladdens your heart as you read it.

Look Up

It was early dawn when the women came
Bearing the spices towards the tomb.
Their heads were bent in the sorrow of loss,
For their Lord had died on a Roman cross.
Now they came to anoint His body in death,
Their thoughts heavy and sad and their eyes down cast.
"Who will roll the stone away from the door?"
They murmured from hearts which were lonely and sore.

They moved together between the trees,
Their voices were clear in the gentle breeze.
"What will we do with that great stone?
We won't be able to move it alone,
It took strong men to place it there.
What will we do? We'd never dare
To ask the soldiers to roll it away.
We'll have to make haste, it will soon be day."

77

The women moved on towards the tomb,
Their steps unsure in the morning gloom.
Tears blinded their eyes as, with heads bent low
They discussed the events of three days ago.
The arrest, the trial, the death of their Lord
Whom they'd trusted and served and greatly adored.
They lifted their eyes as they reached the tomb,
They could not believe it, where was the stone?

That great, big stone had been rolled away,
Their problem was solved in the light of day,
When they lifted their eyes the stone had gone
And with it their fears; they were not alone.
When we lift our eyes from our problems and sins
And look at our Lord, put our trust in Him,
The 'stones' in our lives will be rolled away.
So look to the Saviour and watch and pray.

Mark 16:4 reads, "And looking up they see that the stone is rolled back, for it was exceeding great."
Amy Carmichael says in 'Edges of His Ways': "The sorrowful women were looking down as they walked. We often do that in sorrow. They were wondering who would roll away the stone. They did not see till they looked up that it had been rolled away."

The Donkey

We bear the mark — the cross upon our backs
Since that one day I never will forget.
I stood at the crossroads at Bethany,
The sun was beating from a clear blue sky,
Some old men nodded in the mid-day heat
When I saw two strange men walk down the street.
As they approached I knew they'd come for me,
That I was chosen — as they set me free.

The old men called, as they untied my rope,
"Who gave you leave to take away the colt?"
"The Lord has need of him", I heard them say.
The old men smiled as they led me away.
Where were they taking me? I did not know,
I only knew I felt compelled to go.
Someone was calling me, had need of me
And so I went with them — left Bethany.

Excited crowds lined both sides of the road
Awaiting someone — then towards me strode
A Man, Who smiled and gently stroked my head.
"No one has ever ridden you", He said,
"But I have chosen you to carry Me
To-day along this road from Bethany
Towards a cross upon Mount Calvary
And ever after wear the marks for Me".

78

His followers placed their coats upon my back
And many more were laid along the track
That day I carried Jesus through the crowds
Who waved palm branches high, and cried aloud,
"Hosanna in the Highest — praise the King.
Hosanna in the Highest — let it ring.
Hosanna to the King, Who is the Lord.
Hosanna", still they cried, along the road.

Yes — they hailed Him as their King, that joyous day.
But later in that week they changed their cry
To, "Crucify Him, crucify that Man".
And watched Him die, nailed by His feet and hands.
Not understanding that He was God's Son
Sent to this world, that men might be forgiven
The sin that separates them from the Lord,
'Til they repent and trust the Living Word.

Mary Magdalene

Mark 16:9

Who will roll the stone from my dear Lord's tomb?
Was Mary's thought, as she came, in the early dawn,
To the quiet garden where He had been laid
Three days ago; she was very afraid
As she quietly slipped through the tall, green trees.
What will I do, what will happen to me?
Tears blinded her eyes; "What will I do?" she softly said,
"Now that my Saviour, my dear Lord, is dead."

Mary's thoughts wandered back to that wonderful day
When she'd knelt before Christ on that dusty way.
She'd been plagued with illness, most of her life,
Possessed by devils, by inner strife,
Then Peter had told her of Jesus, the Lord,
Who had healed a young servant, just by speaking a word.
She had met Him, He healed her and set her free,
And now, He was dead, crucified on a tree.

Mary lifted her head as she came to His grave.
Where, where was the stone? She trembled, amazed
That great stone had gone, had been rolled away.
What had happened here? Then she heard a voice say,
"Why seek ye the living among the dead?
Come, see the place where His body was laid,
The Lord is not here, He has risen, He's gone."
Confused and bewildered, Mary turned from the tomb.

Through the garden she stumbled, eyes blinded with tears.
Then a figure appeared from the shadowy trees.
Mary was startled; Who could it be?
A gardener perhaps? Or, could it be He?
Could it be Jesus? She fell on her knees.
"Mary", He said. She could hardly believe it.
Her Lord, Who'd been dead, crucified,
Buried there in that grave, now was alive.
She was no longer alone, He'd risen, the whole world to save.

Mary Magdalene must have loved the Lord very much and her sorrow and loss brought her to the tomb that first Easter morning. She was rewarded by being the first person to see the risen Lord.

Three Rusty Nails

John 20:25

The nails had lain, forgotten, red with rust,
Hidden from sight, covered in mounds of dust
Upon a shelf, there, on the carpenter's stall
Which stood across the road from Pilate's hall.
They were too big and long for his fine work,
And so, they lay there, useless, in the dirt.

The old man saw the crowds passing that day.
They pushed and shoved each other in the way.
He'd heard, the soldiers had arrested Christ
Sometime during the darkness of the night.
They'd dragged Him to the High Priest, first of all,
And now, He stood on trial in Pilate's hall.

The old man's thoughts were sad and far away,
Recalling how He'd met the Christ one day.
He'd come, with His disciples, up the street,
Wearied by walking, He had found a seat
There, in the shade, beside the old man's stall.
And that was the beginning of it all.

The Christ had spoken as He sat at rest.
Admired his tools, all of the very best
He could afford; a good workman he'd been,
All of his life, a carpenter, keen
To bring beauty from a piece of wood.
He'd prospered; people knew his work was good.

Jesus had lifted a carving of a lamb,
Had held it, lovingly, between His hands.
He'd called Himself, 'the Lamb of God', that day,
He'd smiled at him and gone upon His way.
Since then, the old man's soul had been at peace
Because he'd met and talked, that day, with Christ.

The old man's thoughts were broken by a shout.
He saw a Roman soldier running out
Of Pilate's courtyard, straight across the road.
Towards him and his stall he strode,
"I want three nails, quickly, three large, strong nails,"
He shouted at the old man, weak and frail.

With trembling hands, the old man searched around
Among the dusty shavings, 'till he found
The rusty nails, sharp pointed, very long.
"Just right", the soldier said, "here, take this coin,
It surely is enough for me to pay
To hold that Jew upon His cross, today."

The old man caught the coin the soldier tossed,
Not quite believing him about 'a cross'.
But then, the soldier joked about the nails,
How they would hold a body, without fail.
"Please, let me buy them back", the old man pled.
The soldier laughed, and slowly shook his head.

"The crowd has chosen Barabbas, not the Christ,
Listen, they're calling now for Jesus' death."
The soldier went, the old man left his stall
And, trembling, took the road past Pilate's hall,
Along the street and up the stony way,
The path the Christ must take to Calvary.

He hadn't long to wait; he heard their jeers
Long before any of the crowd appeared.
Then came the Lord, dragging the heavy cross,
The soldiers round Him; he was at a loss
To know how best to help his burdened Lord.
How was he going to make Him hear his words?

As Jesus drew abreast of him He stopped,
Unable to carry, further, that great cross.
The carpenter stooped down to wipe His brow,
"I'm sorry Lord — the nails — I didn't know."
His stammering tongue fell silent, as he heard
The Saviour whisper, "I am the Lamb of God."

The nails, which held the Saviour to that tree,
Were nails of sin, driven by you, by me.
Our Saviour turned them into nails of love
As He hung there, praying to God above
For sinners everywhere, for me, for you,
"Father forgive, they know not what they do."
Beside the throne the Lamb of God now stands,
We'll know Him by the nailprints in His hands.

One Sunday morning when listening to Downtown Radio's programme 'Reflections', I heard the song 'Three Rusty Nails' played. I thought that the story would make an interesting poem. My imagination has 'embroidered' it quite a bit.

Barabbas

Matt. 27:15—23

He died to-day, that Man from Galilee.
They crucified Him there on Calvary.
I watched the soldiers nail Him to the cross,
I listened to the women wail their loss,
I saw the darkness creep across the sky
And in my place I saw the Saviour die.

I'd spent my life amongst a band of thieves,
But in my youth, you'll hardly this believe,
John Baptist was my friend, I knew him well,
He was a character, he used to tell me I was lost
Unless I changed my ways, I should repent
And serve God all my days.

I must admit, I thought it was a joke,
Although my friend, he was a funny bloke,
He roamed the hills around Lake Galilee,
He wore queer clothes, ate honey from wild bees,
And taught the crowds they must their sins repent,
Believe in God, and in the One He'd sent.

My friends and I hid out among the hills,
The Romans called us rebels, for we killed
And plundered in the countryside around,
They threw in prison those of us they found.
We recognised no laws but those we made,
Of neither God nor man were we afraid.

One day the news came, Herod had killed John.
He was my friend, whom I relied upon,
It seemed to me I'd nothing left in life
But robbery and killing, sin and strife.
Then I was caught, the sentence passed was death,
I had no hope, no peace, no God, no faith.

In jail I heard that something was afoot,
The Pharisees and Priests had planned to put to death
Upon a cross the Man called Christ
And have the crowd demand I be released;
Many believed He was the Son of God,
The Priests accused Him, calling Him a fraud.

Within my cell I heard the crowd's wild cry,
"Release Barabbas, Jesus crucify"
    The soldiers dragged me roughly up the stairs,
A Man was standing, His beaten body bared,
A crown of thorns was jammed upon His head,
His brow was dripping with the blood He'd shed.

The soldiers laid the cross upon His back,
I watched Him drag it up the stony track.
He stumbled underneath the heavy tree,
I reached His side, He turned His gaze on me,
I looked into His eyes, such love was there,
My stony heart was touched, my soul laid bare.

So now, I know, He suffered there for me,
He took my place that I could be set free.
He whispered His forgiveness for my sin,
And from to-day I've given my life to Him.
And for you too His precious blood was shed,
In love upon the cross your debt He paid.
Oh, give your life to Him and you will be
Forgiven, redeemed, by Christ of Calvary.

Pilate's Wife

Matthew 27:19—37

I knew, that day, that something was afoot.
Pilate was worried, rushing in and out
Interviewing Jews, scribes and Pharisees,
Their priests coming and going secretly.
Rumours were rife here, in Jerusalem,
Conflicting stories spread all about Him,
The Man, Whom all the hub-bub was about,
Jesus from Galilee, without a doubt.

I'd heard about this Jesus from my maid,
A lovely little Jewish girl. She'd said,
He'd lived in Nazareth for many years,
But lately, He had travelled far and near
Preaching to all about the love of God,
Whom He called Father; many called Him, Lord.
Crowds followed Him and listened to His Words.
Many were healed, blind had their sight restored.

I'd heard so much about this Jesus Christ
That I disguised myself and late at night,
Slipped out, with Miriam, my maid,
And joined a crowd going along the road
To Bethany; and there I heard Him speak
Such words of love to all who came to seek
His help and healing; I was greatly moved.
To me, His claim to be God's Son, was proved.

83

Now, all these Jews were calling for His death.
He'd been arrested, brought here, late at night.
And so, my husband, Pilate, was involved
Because he was the Roman governor.
I'd had a dream, a really bad nightmare
About this holy Man and tried to share
My fears with Pilate but I was too late,
He'd given in, left Jesus to his fate.

That awful crowd kept crying, "Crucify,
Release Barabbas, send that Man to die."
Pilate gave in and washed his hands of blame.
I watched and listened, feeling very shamed
That Pontius Pilate should have joined with men
Who'd laughed and jeered and beaten Christ and then,
Jammed on His head a crown of thorns and cried,
"Hail, King of the Jews", and had Him crucified.

Pilate put up a sign, 'King of the Jews,'
Above the cross on Calvary and refused
To change it when the priests complained.
But now, he walks the floor, nervous and strained,
Knowing, the Man, Whom he condemned to die,
Was Jesus Christ, the Son of God, and that I'd
Warned him but he failed to heed
My words and now, it is too late; the Christ is dead.

My little maid came to me late tonight.
Her tears had gone, her face, smiling and bright.
She said that Jesus was alive, not dead.
Many had seen Him, remembering that He'd said
He'd rise again on the third day; and I, a Roman, not a Jew,
Believe that every word is true.
But now, what can I do but strive
To help my husband, Pilate, understand, Christ is alive.

His Robe

John 13:1—17

We had gathered all together in that upper room.
It was Passover and Jesus knew that soon
It would be time for His betrayal and His death.
He'd sent us out, that afternoon, to meet, by stealth,
A man, carrying a pitcher full of water in the street.
We followed him, and reached this house and greeted him
With Jesus' words, "Where is the guest room where we may
Prepare for Christ, the Passover today?"

84

All of us knew that this Passover was going to be
No ordinary meal for our dear Lord and we could see,
During the last few weeks, that He was going through
Some powerful struggle; in His private words to us we knew
That death was in His mind, His death; how could our Lord be killed?
The very thought was foreign to our minds so filled
With dreams of following Jesus Christ to victory
Here on this earth and we, His followers, sharing in His glory.

We all sat down, we'd had a busy day,
And then, our dearest Friend, our Lord stood up and laid
Aside His robe and took a towel, wrapped it round Himself
And, as we looked at Him in wonder and surprise, He knelt
Before each one of us and then began to wash our feet.
He came to me, I couldn't move there in my seat;
"You'll never wash my feet, dear Lord", I rashly said,
As there before me knelt the Son of God with bended head.

My Saviour turned His eyes to mine and I could see
The pain and sorrow in their depths because of me.
"Not my feet only Lord, but hands and head as well".
"That man is clean", He said, "within whose heart I dwell.
For I have shown you here, this night, that you must do,
As I have done, to others; you must follow too,
The path that I, your Master, Friend and Lord have shown.
As servants, follow me, for you are not alone".

The Son of God stood up and took His robe again
As we sat there, wrapped in the silence and the calm
Of thought of this example He had left for us.
We did not know His robe would lie beneath a cross,
Where He would die to save all men from sin and shame.
Show them the only way through suffering and pain,
And so provide another robe for man to wear,
The Robe of Righteousness that all His Sons may share.

8/
2

THE NEW WINDMILL SERIES
General Editors: Anne and Ian Serraillier

60

BLACK NARCISSUS

This sensitive and highly dramatic tale
of a small group of nuns who try to
establish themselves in an evil-haunted
palace in the Himalayas will appeal to
older readers, especially girls.